# Possible Worlds of Fiction and History

# Possible Worlds of Fiction and History

*The Postmodern Stage*

Lubomír Doležel

The Johns Hopkins University Press
*Baltimore*

Printed in the United States of America on acid-free paper
9 8 7 6 5 4 3 2 1

The Johns Hopkins University Press
2715 North Charles Street
Baltimore, Maryland 21218-4363
www.press.jhu.edu

Library of Congress Cataloging-in-Publication Data
Doležel, Lubomír.
Possible worlds of fiction and history : the postmodern stage / Lubomír Doležel.
p. cm.
Includes bibliographical references and index.
ISBN-13: 978-0-8018-9463-3 (acid-free paper)
ISBN-10: 0-8018-9463-8 (acid-free paper)
1. Historical fiction—History and criticism. 2. Postmodernism (Literature). I. Title.
PN3441.D65 2010
809.3—dc22 2009027093

A catalog record for this book is available from the British Library.



The Johns Hopkins University Press uses environmentally friendly book materials, including recycled text paper that is composed of at least 30 percent post-consumer waste, whenever possible. All of our book papers are acid-free, and our jackets and covers are printed on paper with recycled content.

# CONTENTS

# PREFACE

Hayden White proclaimed that "historical texts are literary artifacts" (1978; see also White 1999, 4), and thus he legitimized the participation of theorists of literature in the debate about the status and aims of historical inquiry. Indeed, they were debating even before 1978, first in Roland Barthes's well-known 1967 paper. Almost simultaneously, in 1968, Frank Kermode wrote: "It seems . . . that philosophy of history is the business of those who teach novels" (qtd. in Vann 1995, 40). A positive consequence of this "linguistic turn" was that the historian's alliances were broadened, or, rather, redirected—from sociology, geography, political science, and other social sciences to literary studies, narratology, linguistics, discourse analysis, and text theory. New, until then unreflected aspects of historical writing came under scrutiny. I believe, however, that the historians and the theorists of history have been fed a restricted and one-sided diet by their new companions. Opinions and theories supporting White's claim have been given prominence. I cannot resist the temptation to dissent from this "official" view. And although I do not have the authority to speak as a historian or for them, I do want them to know that the literary theoretical front is not as homogeneous as the postmodern establishment has presented it to be.

The "postmodern challenge" to the foundations of history as a cognitive activity led, in Brian Fay's words, "to the vehement public debate carried on in the mass media as well as professional journals about the nature of history as a discipline" (1998, 1). At the center of this debate is the relationship between history and fiction. Indeed, to quote Fay again, in the postmodern period "the question 'how is history like and unlike fiction?' replaced 'how is history like and unlike science?' as the guiding question of metahistorical reflection" (2). In my book *Heterocosmica: Fiction and Possible Worlds* (1998) I elaborated a theory of fiction based on the interdisciplinary framework of possible worlds. At the time it seemed natural to explore what this possible-worlds semantics of fiction could say about the relationship of fiction and history. The readers of *Heterocosmica* will easily recognize that my contribution to the fiction-history debate is not based on a new theory but is a new application of possible-worlds semantics. Surprisingly, this application has not been tested; no meticulous study of the fruitfulness of this concept for the theory of history is available. When Sture Allén convened the interdisciplinary Nobel Symposium 65 in 1986 (for the proceedings, see Allén, ed., 1989), specialists from linguistics, literary theory, art history, quantum physics, cosmology, and so on, had the opportunity to exchange views on the theoretical utility of possible worlds for their disciplines. However, except for historians of science, no historian was present at the symposium.

Since we do not know for sure whether postmodernism is now dead or dying or still dominating the literary and cultural scene (see Bertens 1997, 3–4), in this book I try to pursue two goals: First, it is an argument in the postmodern debate on metahistory; this aim predominates in the theoretical chapters, I and II. Second, it is a contribution to the emerging history of postmodernism, an aim that is prevalent in the analytical chapters, III–V. To provide a context for the book's theme, I wrote an introduction summarizing some concepts and trends of postmodernism. Needless to say, this delineation is neither exhaustive nor systematic.

Chapters I and II present the postmodern thesis that there is no fundamental difference between the fictional and the historical narrative. My counterargument starts with the admission that this thesis applies to the discourse (textual) level of narrative. I continue, however, by pointing out that the postmodern thesis can be subverted if we shift from the level of discourse to the level of worlds. Both fiction and historiography construct possible worlds. However, in their modes of construction, in their functions, and in their structural and semantic properties the two kinds of possible worlds show fundamental differences. The possible-worlds framework enables us to reassert the status of historiography as an activity of *noesis:* its possible worlds are models of the actual past. Fiction making is an activity of *poiesis:* fictional worlds are imaginary possible alternatives to the actual world.

I pursue this distinction not only on the theoretical level but also by analyzing a corpus of fictional and historical texts. I could have selected works from various periods for this analysis, but I found postmodern fictional and historical writings to be most useful for discussing a postmodern theoretical problem. They allow us to study the mutual exchange between the challenging theory and the parallel writing practice. I shall try to answer two recurring questions: how were the fiction and history writing of the postmodern era affected by the postmodern metahistory? and what general theoretical insights are afforded by a careful analysis of history and fiction of the postmodern era? These texts are relevant also because their authors are usually well aware of the postmodern challenge and provide their own arguments for or against it.

I have worked on this book for more than ten years. During these years I have profited from discussions with the students in my seminars at the University of Toronto and at Masaryk University, in Brno, Czech Republic, and with colleagues at these institutions, as well as at several scholarly gatherings, such as the Stockholm conference on representation and perspective and the seminar on possible worlds at the Université de Paris–Jussieu. I am especially grateful to Peter Nesselroth, who shared with me his profound knowledge and understanding of the complex, often obscure postmodern thought, and to Andrew Lass, who made invaluable comments on the manuscript from his interdisciplinary perspective. Nancy H. Traill, my longtime language adviser, deserves my gratitude for reading the whole manuscript and suggesting changes to my wording, thus giving me the confidence that the book is written in cultivated English. A special note of thanks goes to the anonymous reader who in his recommendation to the Johns Hopkins University Press expressed high appreciation of my work and made inspiring suggestions, in addition to correcting numerous typing errors. In the final preparation of the manuscript, I needed a computer expert with an eagle eye; my daughter Milena and especially my copy editor, Joanne Allen, performed this service, and I owe them my thanks.

# Possible Worlds of Fiction and History

# Remarks on Postmodernism

To date there is no consensus about what postmodernism is or was. The problem might be that it is a phenomenon of vast scope and diversity, with an impact on all forms of culture—architecture, the arts, literature, mass media, lifestyle. For the purposes of this study we need no more than an orientation in this complex and overworked subject. I will be guided by a few recognized experts on postmodernism in establishing a context in which the central problem of this book can better be understood.

## 1. Postmodernism as a Period Style

Let us first consider whether postmodernism is a period style or a perennial alternative trend of cultural history. Umberto Eco leads those who consider postmodernism to be an atemporal way of thinking and representation: "I believe that postmodernism is not a trend to be chronologically defined, but, rather, an ideal category—or better still, a *Kunstwollen*, a way of operating. We could say that every period has its own postmodernism, just as every period would have its own mannerism (and, in fact, I wonder if postmodernism is not the modern name for mannerism as a metahistorical category)" (1983, 66). Linda Hutcheon maintains that a positioning of postmodernism in time "is not terribly useful" (1988, 4). Aron Kibédi-Varga is not quite sure: "The term 'modernity' refers to a historical era of a certain duration, and which can be subdivided into various periods. On the contrary, the term 'postmodernity,' if it is used to refer to a period and not as a conceptual notion, can only refer to something still very new and brief" (1988, 29).

But more than two decades have elapsed since these statements were printed, and postmodernism is no longer "something still very new and brief." It has become an international movement, and therefore its chronology, as Douwe Fokkema argues, "is not only a matter of when, but also of where, since the introduction and eventual demise of postmodernism did not take place synchronically in all literatures of this world" (1997, 24). Fokkema limits his analysis of postmodernist strategies and devices to "a selection of texts which appeared roughly between 1960 and 1980, in North America and elsewhere in the world. . . . However, 1980 is not the end of postmodernism. With twists and turns, the narrative and stylistic devices of postmodernism as well as their semantic correlates have lived on, were absorbed and promulgated in new social-historical contexts, became intertwined with different traditions, and dissipated only when they were superseded by new interests" (26).[1] In this view, postmodernism, like cultural and artistic movements of the past, is a period in time rather than a timeless cultural phenomenon. Quite commonly we place Romanticism in the first decades of the nineteenth century, art nouveau at the *fin de siècle,* the avant-gardes in the 1920s and 1930s. We speak about pre-Romanticism and, indeed, of post-modernism using chronological labels.

The emergence of postmodernism is marked by the rejection of all authority. This rejection was expressed most vocally in 1968, the year in which all political, cultural, and moral dogmas were shattered. Although the radical political goals of 1968 were not achieved, what followed, at least in Western societies, was a period of unprecedented political and personal freedom.[2] It has been a golden age for writing because restrictions on free speech could no longer be upheld and in the "new world" of cyberspace are not even enforceable. Never again hemlock for Socrates, exile for Ovid, stake for Giordano Bruno, trial for Flaubert, prison for Havel. When the walls protecting propriety came down, all the taboos of the margins flooded "high" art, literature, and culture: the Gothic, the fantastic, the grotesque, the popular, and the vulgar, pornography, unspeakable horrors and perverse pleasures, heretic morality, and unofficial history. The rejected taboos blended with lofty traditions of the past, creating a "mumbo-jumbo" mixture, ready to be playfully shaped like images in a kaleidoscope.

Is postmodernism now over, or is it still alive in today's world? It is too early to tell. Some think that it was overthrown by a mimetic counter-revolution, never having been able to destroy mimesis totally. Maybe it was outsmarted by the computer, a logocentric machine par excellence.

It may have withered because since 9/11 the world has not been a propitious place for postmodern playing. We should not be terribly bothered by this uncertainty. Chronological boundaries are always fuzzy, and we are still too close to postmodernism to see the present as anything but a time of cultural crisis.

Aware of the historicity of postmodernism, we part company with its propagandists, who claim to be witnessing "the end of history," "the final stage of philosophy," "the last artistic accomplishment." Postmodernism, like every cultural movement since Romanticism, started as a provocative heresy but achieved the status of a historical era. It is neither an ephemeral fad nor a millennium. We are wiser because of its cultural critique, because of its ruthless deconstruction of all authority. We are wiser because we think and act with much less certainty.

## 2. Plays of Contradictions

The conception of postmodernism that is closest to a possible-worlds semantics is Brian McHale's thesis about postmodern fiction. McHale defines postmodern fiction in sharp contrast to its modern predecessor: modernism is dominated by epistemological concerns, postmodernism by ontological ones: "Modernist fiction deploys strategies which engage and foreground questions such as . . . 'How can I interpret this world of which I am a part? And what am I in it?' Other typical modernist questions might be added: What is there to be known?; Who knows it?; How do they know it, and with what degree of certainty?; How is knowledge transmitted from one knower to another, and with what degree of reliability?; How does the object of knowledge change as it passes from knower to knower?; What are the limits of the knowable?" (1987, 9). In contrast, "postmodernist fiction deploys strategies which engage and foreground questions like . . . : 'Which world is this? What is to be done in it? Which of my selves is to do it?' Other typical postmodernist questions bear either on the ontology of the literary text itself or on the ontology of the world which it projects, for instance: What is a world?; What kinds of world are there, how are they constituted, and how do they differ?; What happens when different kinds of world are placed in confrontation, or when boundaries between worlds are violated?" (9–10).

McHale's thesis about postmodern fiction can be generalized in two ways. First, the focus on ontological issues is characteristic not only of postmodern fiction but of postmodern writing and culture in general. Postmodernism can be characterized as an epoch-making ontological experiment, an experiment in world creation, world deconstruction, world fusion.[3] Second, not only ontological but all kinds of boundaries—between modes of writing, types of discourse and text, natural and supernatural worlds, noetic (cognitive) and poietic (creative) activity—are questioned, crossed, or erased in postmodern culture. Crossing boundaries has become a pastime of postmodernists and their epigones.

Linda Hutcheon is a stimulating theorist of postmodernism; while her discourse is postmodern, it is monitored by a keen and incorruptible intellect.[4] In her view, postmodernism is an accumulation of contradictions, paradoxes being its most radical manifestation: "Postmodernism is a contradictory phenomenon, one that uses and abuses, installs and then subverts, the very concepts it challenges—be it in architecture, literature, painting, sculpture, film, video, dance, TV, music, philosophy, aesthetic theory, psychoanalysis, linguistics, or historiography" (1988, 4). Postmodern thinking, represented by Jean-François Lyotard, Michel Foucault, and others, "is typically paradoxical": their theories are "masterful denials of mastery, . . . cohesive attacks on cohesion, . . . essentializing challenges to essences" (20). Postmodernism does not reject the cultural past; it absorbs it as one pole into its paradigm of contradictions. In this integration, the past is subject to complex reprocessings, reinterpretations, restructurings.

The contradictions that according to Hutcheon represent the crux of postmodernism cannot be resolved by logical means. They are tensions that stimulate and nurture playing. The concept of play is crucial to the original postmodern theorizing. Derrida, having acknowledged that it was Lévi-Strauss who "has brought to light the play of repetition and the repetition of play," expresses the crucial role of playing in postmodern thinking about contradictions: "Play is always a play of absence and presence, but if it is to be thought radically, play must be conceived of before the alternative of presence and absence" (1996, 447). Now we can understand better the nature of postmodern ontology. The "epoch-making experiment" in world construction, deconstruction, and fusion is play with possible worlds. Postmodernism creates a wonderland where each thing can morph into another, a ludic world free of conventions, rules, and traditions.[5]

Postmodern ludic strategy proceeds in three steps: undermine (deconstruct) all boundaries and oppositions; create spaces of fusion, blends, collages; do not resolve contradictions but let all flowers, however incompatible, however disharmonious, bloom in one and the same garden bed.

It is no coincidence that metaphors of play and game are very common both in postmodern artistic and literary practice and in its theorizing. The ludic spirit, which probably was last so vital in the rococo, is not frivolous but creative. The rococo enriched the world with remarkable, lasting artifacts: the white churches of Bavaria, the music of Mozart, the paintings of Watteau. The ludic spirit of postmodernism liberated architecture from stern modernist boxes, visual arts from the dominion of abstraction, literature from the last constraints of mimetism, and historiography from dogmatic, arrogant positivism.

## 3. Playing in a Serious World

If playing is the main activity of the postmodernists, the question naturally arises how it can be reconciled with established modes of inquiry and serious ideological activities. This is a fundamental question for every discipline that acquires, accumulates, and interprets information about the world. The most radical, usually later, postmodernists propose a solution to this dilemma by propagating *endism.* According to the dogma of endism, postmodern ludic philosophy, with its rejection of logocentrism and with its semantics of *différance,* has brought an end to cognitive activities, the end of historiography, of science, of philosophy. The second, less radical solution to the dilemma is to transform established cognitive and ideological activities by putting them on new ontological and epistemological foundations. As we shall see, this transformation has most profoundly affected literary study (see below, sec. 5) and historiography (see chapter I). Finally, there is within the postmodern paradigm a moderate trend that acknowledges that new, experimental modes of literary, historical, philosophical, and other writing are possible, indeed necessary, but resists jettisoning well-tested foundational principles (see chapters III and V). This trend, I believe, is a prefigurement of new post-postmodern developments, one that I hope will one day be valued as postmodern thought's main contribution to cultural history.

These three trends demonstrate that postmodernism, like any well-developed cultural movement, is not homogeneous. It has shifting dominants, shifting margins, and temporary *poputchiks* (fellow travelers). It also radiates outside its own domain to influence or attract other cultural movements. Owing to certain strong sociohistorical factors a whole gamut of ideological trends emerged during the postmodern period. Fokkema enumerates five such kinds of writing: feminist writing, historiographic fiction, postcolonial fiction, autobiographical writing, and fiction focusing on cultural identity. He also aligns himself with the widely held opinion that "postmodernism . . . contradicts political commitment" (1987, 234). Hutcheon is also skeptical: "The postmodern may offer art as the site of political struggle by its posing of multiple and deconstructing questions, but it does not seem to be able to make the move into political agency" (1989, 157).

The opinion that the postmodernists are not interested in political activism is held widely but not universally. With respect to feminism Susan Suleiman points to the mutual intertwining and enrichment that the alliance with postmodernism can bring: "The alliance of feminists and postmodernists has a plainly political significance. . . . 'Feminism' brings to postmodernism the political guarantee postmodernism needs to feel respectable as an avant-garde practice" (qtd. in Fokkema 1997, 31). Perhaps Suleiman has in mind the nondogmatic, nonmilitant feminism, the liberation philosophy in the tradition of avant-garde's political commitments.

In contrast to such friends of postmodernism as Suleiman, many feminists, including Seyla Benhabib, do not accept what Benhabib describes as "the contemporary alliance between feminism and postmodernism" (1996, 540). Summarizing the basic theses of postmodernism concerning "the end of the episteme of representation," Benhabib argues that "the strong postmodernist position is incompatible with, and in fact renders incoherent feminism as a theoretical articulation of a struggling social movement" (544). "Postmodernism," writes Benhabib, "undermines the feminist commitment to women's agency and sense of selfhood, to the reappropriation of women's own history in the name of an emancipated future, and the exercise of radical social criticism which uncovers gender 'in all its endless variety and monotonous similarity'" (553). We should recall Hutcheon's observation that in spite of all the political undertones or overtones of postmodernism, the postmodernists are hesitant to undertake any political action. The postmodernists' deconstruction of all authority can appeal to the "liberation ideologies" of their contemporaries, but on the barricades they would never receive from these critics of authority more than cheerleaders' support.

## 4. Philosophy of Language

The philosophy of Jacques Derrida is both the inspiration for and the crowning of postmodernism. Derrida proceeds within the well-known framework of the twentieth-century "linguistic turn" in philosophy. Although different, indeed contradictory philosophical trends have operated within this framework—"ordinary language" philosophy, analytical philosophy, and deconstruction—they share the belief that all ancient philosophical problems, metaphysical, ontological, epistemological, axiological, ethical, and so on, can be resolved by analyzing language. The notion of language substituted and superseded such notions as world, consciousness, mind, thinking, and acting. Thus, language is no longer a tool of diverse human faculties and activities. In the best case, it stands as a barrier between the world and human consciousness; in the worst case, it is a "prison house" from which there is no escape, a monstrous power of blindness for which there is no cure. Postmodern thought can be best characterized as radical linguistic determinism.

Derrida claims that his philosophy of language is derived from Ferdinand de Saussure's semiotic theory of language. According to Saussure, language is not a passive means for designating entities of the world. Languages have their own structures, independent of the structures of the world. Language is an active system of signification, imposing its own grid on the world. A "nomenclature" view of language, one that sees language as "a list of terms each corresponding to a thing," is primitive, pretheoretical. A linguistic theory has to bracket the extralinguistic relationship of reference—the relationship of signs to objects—and explore the intralinguistic relationship of the two aspects of the sign, signifier and signified, which are united not by a natural bond of similarity but by convention. The foundation of language is arbitrariness; it is in the arbitrary interplay of signifiers and signifieds that language generates meaning.

Derrida pushes Saussure's semantics and semiotics beyond their limits (see Doležel 1990, 114). He radicalizes the concept of arbitrariness by creating new signifiers or new combinations of signifiers to express new philosophical categories, a meaning production typical of poetry. He also radicalizes the divorce of language from the world: not only is the reference relation bracketed but it is not a part of Derrida's semantics of natural language. A free-floating language sign produces meaning only by self-reference, by the relationship of signs to signs. Linguistic meaning can be expressed solely by substituting one sign for another sign. As in a unilingual dictionary, the meaning of a word can be given only by another word, and so on, in an infinite regress of *différance*. Language becomes a self-propelled generator of world- and subject-independent meaning.

Armed with this radical philosophy of language, Derrida attacks the very foundations of Western philosophy. One pillar of this philosophy is the metaphysics of presence; the other, logocentrism. The first traditional axiom claims that there is a world existing independently of language, independently of any representation. The second axiom claims that the world can be recognized, described, analyzed, and understood through rational discourse. According to Jonathan Culler (who explains lucidly the often obtuse discourse of deconstructionist philosophy), the "basic project" of logocentrism is that of determining "the nature of truth, reason, being, and of distinguishing the essential from the contingent, the well-grounded from the factitious" (1982, 151). It is not difficult to recognize that logocentrism is the epistemology of science, and consequently it is the foundation of science that deconstruction puts into question.

I have stated that postmodernism is a colossal ontological experiment, a play with world construction. It is no wonder, then, that in the postmodern paradigm Derrida's radical linguistic skepticism is coupled with radical philosophical constructivism. The principle of radical philosophical constructivism, expressed by Nelson Goodman, is quite simple: "We can have words without a world but no world without words or other symbols" (1978, 6). Words do not describe or represent a world; they construct it. Philosophical constructivism gives us no indication how words could exist without a world, or more specifically, without a being who actually exists in a world and utters words. (I return to this problem in chapter II.)

Many people think that living in a Derridian world would be closer to a nightmare than to a utopia.[6] If we had only self-referential language at our disposal, we would lack the most important tool for talking about the world and ourselves, for establishing and maintaining human relationships, for acquiring knowledge. In an anti-logocentric world, from which rationality would be expelled, we would not be able to tell the difference between true and false statements, between who is trustworthy and who is a liar, between who is innocent and who is guilty, between what is genuine and what is fake. Would it be an anarchistic paradise or lawless, destructive chaos?

We could speculate about this question, but I find it more fruitful to offer an alternative, theoretically more productive and pragmatically more optimistic vision of the triangle person-language-world. This epistemological position, which I develop in chapter II, is derived from human cognitive endowment. This endowment does not afford a total and absolutely certain knowledge—humans are not omniscient—but rather a knowledge restricted by two limits. The upper limit is the impossibility to utter magic performatives. By *magic performative* I mean a piece of language that, when uttered, produces an actual-world entity (see II.1). No human has this ability. The lower limit of human cognitive endowment is set by the impossibility of not discriminating. It is impossible for a human being not to discriminate between a tree and a cloud. It is impossible for a human being not to ask, is this true or false? Between these two impossibilities lie the cognitive possibilities of human beings as members of a particular species.

## 5. Deconstructive Criticism and Applied Grammatology

I have indicated what options the postmodern ludic thought had when faced with serious cognitive activities. One such activity, the activity we call variously "literary criticism," "literary theory," and "literary interpretation," among other terms, was very early and very strongly influenced by postmodern thought. Often, the postmodern impact on humanistic, historical, and anthropological fields of inquiry is presented as an attack by literary critics on the foundations of these disciplines. The postmodern challenge to the integrity of history is, speaking somewhat simplistically, an attempt to replace history by fictional literature (see chapter I).

Despite the popularity of views that see postmodern literary criticism as the fifth column invading peace-loving neighbors, I believe that this reconstruction of events is distorted. We should distinguish between deconstruction as an epistemological position and deconstruction as a practice of poetological and aesthetic analysis. If we accept the view that literature is an aesthetic phenomenon—a view prevalent in all forms of European thinking about literature at least since Russian formalism—then we can see the postmodern, poststructuralist conception of literature and literary analysis as an aggressive elaboration of structuralist aesthetics and poetics.

Deconstruction as epistemology makes radical claims,[7] but its poetological practice does not (and perhaps cannot) fully comply with these theoretical claims. This imbalance is especially apparent in the work of J. Hillis Miller, who is both a theorist and a practitioner of deconstructive criticism. As a theorist, Miller states what the deconstructive critic should do; as a practitioner he demonstrates what this critic actually does.

Miller's theoretical program posits a sharp contrast between poststructuralism and structuralism. The structuralists are "Socratic, theoretical or canny critics, . . . lulled by the promise of a rational ordering of literary study on the basis of solid advances in scientific knowledge about language." The poststructuralist critics are "rigorously sane and rational," but they are alert to the fact that "the thread of logic leads . . . into regions which are alogical, absurd. . . . In fact the moment when logic fails in their work is the moment of their deepest penetration into the actual nature of literary language, or of language as such" (1976, 335–38; cf. Culler 1982, 23).

Clearly, Miller distances himself from the structuralists on general epistemological grounds. This motivation becomes even more evident in his polemical engagement with one of them, Shlomith Rimmon-Kenan: "Structuralism . . . is reasoned, more or less abstract, given to diagrams and tables. It is written from within an international community of researchers sharing the same goals, the same norms and procedures, and speaking the same language of analysis." It is incorporated "within a larger domain of linguistics and other 'human sciences,' those in turn within a larger domain including the social and physical sciences, as part of a world-wide collective enterprise of technicalization and scientific mastery. . . . The goal of 'deconstruction' is very different from this. The system of assumptions defining the collective enterprise of scientific mastery is one of the things it wants to put in question by disarticulating it or by showing that it disarticulates itself. This means showing that it contains contradictions and aporias making its enterprise impossible" (Miller 1980–81, 189, 190). This rather long quote is useful in that it sets out the contrary positions very clearly and uncompromisingly. In another context, when Miller contrasts poststructuralism with New Criticism, he maintains that the New Critics strove for "organic unity," for "total and totalizable significance" of literary texts, while the deconstructivists claim that literary texts are "unreadable." "Unreadability," he explains, "is the generation by the text itself of a desire for the possession of the logos, while at the same time the text frustrates this desire, in a torsion of undecidability which is intrinsic to language" (1980, 112, 113).

But how does an "uncanny" critic go about analyzing "unreadable" texts, and what can he say about them? Observing Miller's engagement with Thomas Hardy's poem "In Front of the Landscape," we see him switching back and forth between two analytical techniques or levels. On the first level, he painstakingly explains the meanings of obscure and polysemic words and phrases in order to produce at the end a prosaic paraphrase of the poem, a summary of its "content," what he calls its "topography": "There is a lot of guilt around somewhere. It is guilt born of betrayal of trust. Both the speaker and the ghosts are suffering intensely for it. Exactly what betrayal is in question for each of the ghosts the reader is not told. He knows only that they were once fair and happy and that the speaker 'fellowed' with them. Later they were betrayed by him or by others, or thought they were betrayed" (1985, 81). On the second level, Miller sees the poem not as paraphrasable content but as a "complex act of translation": "The ghosts and the scenes, objects, episodes . . . are transposed not just into words, but into words architecturally or musically ordered" (84). To reveal the architecture and music of the poem, Miller reconstructs its wavelike rhythmic and rhyming pattern and its "tropography", that is, its dominant poetic (rhetorical) device—prosopopeia overlapping with catachresis (74–75, 86–87).[8] Thus, the second analytical move of the deconstructionist critic dismantles the paraphrase, penetrating beyond the prosaic content to the aesthetic form. In Miller's poetological practice deconstruction is a displacement of the prosaic transcription of poetic texts. As such, it is a challenge to the traditional interpretive practice that strips the -poetic work of its aesthetic features in order to find its message.[9]

Miller's paper was published in the same year as Gregory L. Ulmer's book in which he analyzed Derrida's writings on literature and coined the term *applied grammatology* (Ulmer 1985). Ulmer posits that Derrida treats differently "philosophical works (which he deconstructs) and literary or artistic texts (which he mimes). The methodologies in the two instances bear little resemblance to each other: the philosophical work is treated as an object of study, which is analytically articulated by locating and describing the gap or discontinuity separating what the work 'says' (its conclusions and propositions) from what it 'shows' or 'dis-plays' (its examples, data, the materials with which it, in turn, is working). Literary or plastic texts (a 'new new novel' by Sollers, or drawings by Adami, for example) are not analyzed but are adopted as models or tutors to be imitated, as generative forms for the production of another text" (x–xi).

There is no need here to go into details of Ulmer's analysis of Derrida's writings as inspiration for applied grammatology. Let me just mention that according to Ulmer, Derrida activates the tradition of inscriptions of non-Western cultures and "elaborates a tripartite script—picto-ideo-phonographic—which . . . consists of the following elements: a discursive commentary (the phonetic level); examples interpolated ('pinned') into the discourse (the ideographic element); and 'found' pictorial material" (99).[10]

A very instructive contribution to an understanding of applied grammatology has been recently published by Peter Nesselroth (2007). Proceeding from the general assumption that "writing is capable of producing meaning(s) that are quite independent of the spoken," Nesselroth examines in detail Derrida's readings of Valéry, Ponge, and Joyce, originally presented as lectures. Having lucidly reconstructed these readings,

Nesselroth concludes that "they are not comments made from above to give a clear overall understanding of the text's unity or functioning. Unlike academic essays or professorial presentations, they are actually replays and reenactments of the initial authorial gesture, miming and doubling up on or writing over" (431). The case of the Joyce "replay" is especially revealing: Derrida "captures Joyce's narrative practice and turns it into his own. Joyce becomes his itinerary and destination, his odyssey" (442).

Nesselroth's revelation of Derrida's method clearly shows that applied grammatology is not literary analysis; rather, it is its alternative. It proceeds as creative modeling does; that is, it does not stop at a representation of designs, structures, or laws of the object but proves its validity by actively recreating ("simulating") the modeled object. Derrida's texts are close to rewrites, the supreme manifestations of postmodern intertextuality (see Doležel 1998, 206–26). The cognitive value of these rewrites is in their revelation and demonstration of what Derrida calls "the hidden law of its [the imitated original text's] composition, and the rule of its game" (qtd. in Nesselroth 2007, 443). Literary analysis has attempted to describe these "laws" and "rules" in a theoretical language. Derrida's applied grammatology intuits them and reactivates them in a creative act of a singular poetic text. That is why applied grammatology is effective only when practiced by a poet whose talent is commensurate with that of the original creator. Derrida wisely chooses his literary subjects by "affinity," by a natural closeness of his own poetic talent with the talents of Valéry, Ponge, and Joyce. We can hardly imagine him choosing a nineteenth-century realist for his rewriting.

I believe that applied grammatology, when properly understood and skillfully practiced, constitutes a new branch of the study of literature. As Nesseroth puts it, "This type of writing is not a frivolous, deliberately hermetic, activity. . . . It is a style that blurs the lines of demarcation between literary theory and literature because literary theory is also writing. The two are inevitably and inextricably in each other's margin" (2007, 442). There is no reason to see "logocentric" literary theory and applied grammatology as competitors or even antagonists; the two approaches are complementary. Applied grammatology has enriched the choices offered to the students of literature. What is needed is applied grammatologists whose poetic talent matches that of the master. But whatever the future of the study of literature, it is clear that neither the deconstructive criticism practiced by J. Hillis Miller nor applied grammatology stimulated by Derrida is exportable beyond the confines of literature. These methods are applicable only to those modes of writing that possess aesthetic properties and pursue aesthetic aims.

# The Postmodern Challenge

COUNTLESS ARE THE STORIES [*récits*] of the world." Thus starts the classic work of French structuralist narratology, a celebrated study penned by Roland Barthes (1966). Consequently, the scope of the theory of *récit*, now generally called narratology, became indefinitely large. The "narratological imperialism" rolled over long-established boundaries between text types and genres of writing. In particular, it erased the traditional boundary between fictional and historical narrative. This is the ammunition needed for launching the postmodern challenge to the integrity of history.

## 1. The Fatal Equation

To explain the profound impact of the postmodern challenge, let me briefly summarize two basic assumptions of the modern study of history, one ontological, the other epistemological, which were aptly formulated by François Châtelet in the introduction to his study of the birth of historiography:

> The historical Spirit believes in the reality of the past, and maintains that the past, in its mode of being and, to a certain extent, in its content, is not different in nature from the present. Recognizing what is no longer as having been, he acknowledges that what happened did formerly exist, in a specific time and place, just as what now we see exists. . . . That means, in particular, that it is not in any way acceptable to treat what has happened as fictive, as unreal, and that the nonpresence of the past (and of the future) cannot in any manner be identified with nonreality. (1962, 11; qtd. in Le Goff 1992, 10)
>
> It is indispensable that the past, which is held to be real and decisive, be studied rigorously insofar as past times are considered as

having a claim on our attention, insofar as a structure is assigned to them, insofar as their traces are visible in the present. It is necessary that every discourse concerning the past be able to clearly show why—on the basis of which documents, and what evidence—it proposes a particular sequence of events, a particular version, rather than another. It is especially important that great care be taken in dating and locating the event, since the latter acquires historical status only to the extent that it is determined in this way. (21–22; qtd. in Le Goff 1992, 11)

Only five years after Châtelet's principles were spelled out, Roland Barthes published his essay "Le discours de l'histoire" (1967), in which he undermined these foundations of modern historiography. Barthes proposes to look at historical writing as a type of narrative discourse and from this standpoint to reexamine its relationship to fictional narrative: "Does the narration of past events, which, in our culture from the time of the Greeks onwards, has generally been subject to the sanction of historical 'science,' bound to the unbending standard of the 'real' and justified by the principles of 'rational' exposition—does this narration differ, in some specific trait, in some indubitably pertinent feature, from imaginary narration, as we find it in the epic, the novel, the drama?" (65; 7).[1] At the end of his essay Barthes provides an answer, and this answer is negative.

Barthes's argument draws on two sources: linguistic text theory and the postmodern philosophy of language. We might wonder how a structuralist text theory and a poststructuralist linguistic philosophy can complement and support each other, and indeed they do not. Barthes simply leaps from one to the other.

In his meticulous analysis of the discourse of narrative history Barthes features two classes of textual devices, formal and thematic. To demonstrate Barthes's approach, I shall concentrate on two particularly telling cases: shifters among the formal devices and devices of "personal thematic" among the thematic devices.

Shifters, expressions of shifting deixis (in the wide sense), were first described by Otto Jespersen and named and studied by Roman Jakobson (1957). Following Jakobson's lead, Barthes focuses first on two kinds of shifters in historical discourse. The first kind, shifters of listening, express the historian's connection with his sources or with his personal experience: "as I have heard," "to my knowledge" (66; 8). The second kind of shifters, "the organizers," "provide explicit points of reference in the text" and thus determine the flow of the discourse: "as we have mentioned above," "we will say no more about this, etc." (66–67; 8–9).

The shifters of listening and organizing are indices of discursive subjectivity, traces of authorial interference in the narration; they undermine the highly valued "objectivity" of historical discourse. The issue of discursive objectivity resurfaces in Barthes's discussion of yet another class of shifters, those that refer to the "protagonists of the act of uttering, the receiver and, particularly, the sender." Historical writing cultivates an "absenting" of the sender from his message, which results in "a systematic deficiency of any form of sign referring to the sender of the historical message. The history seems to be telling itself all on its own." *Seems* is the crucial word for Barthes's interpretation of the basic mode of narration—the impersonal *Er*-form authoritative mode (see Doležel 1998, 148–49; and chapter III in this volume)—which the texts of history share with the realistic novel. The objectivity of this mode is, according to Barthes, a "referential illusion." "Today linguistics and psychoanalysis have made us much more lucid with regard to privative utterances: we know that absences of signs are also in themselves significant" (69; 11).

When it comes to the "content units," Barthes is even closer to the structuralist design (partly of his own making), moving from existents (subjects), occurrents (predicates), and indices (modifiers) through Proppian functions to the "personal thematic of the author." His concept of personal thematic, based on recurrent themes—such as *fama* in Tacitus—is a macrostructural trait that is specific to the discourse of individual historians (70; 13). In another move toward discourse macrostructures Barthes distinguishes supraindividual varieties of history, determined by "predominating" features. When "the indexical units predominate," historical narrative is drawn "towards a metaphorical form and borders upon the lyrical and symbolic" (Michelet). "When, by contrast, it is the functional units which predominate in a historian . . . , History takes on a metonymic form and becomes a close relation of the epic" (Thierry). Finally, there is a type of History where reasoning is dominant, and this history is "reflexive," "which we might also call strategic history" (Machiavelli) (72; 15).[2]

Barthes emphasizes repeatedly that the features of narrative discourse that he deals with are shared by historical and fictional narratives. In connection with the classes of content units he writes: "As far as a preliminary sample seems to indicate, classes of this kind are the very same as we have claimed to discover in the fictional narrative," and he refers to his 1966 paper (71; 14). He is quite correct. As far as shifters and content units are concerned, it is difficult to imagine any discourse lacking them. Barthes's discourse analysis is valuable in that it has made evident what most historians have so far neglected: historical writing is discourse; a piece of it is text. Revealing discourse features can lead to very important discoveries about the nature and varieties of historical writing. The analysis of shifters certainly undermines the cherished concept of historical "objectivity," but as readers of any classic historical works can testify, that has been a myth anyway (see II.2). With regard to Barthes's essential question, the relationship between history and fiction, discourse analysis cannot support any particular answer, or rather, it can support any answer.

Perhaps aware of this difficulty, Barthes makes a sharp turn in the last part of his essay. Leaving aside categories of discourse analysis, he answers his question by resorting to the emerging postmodern philosophy of language. He claims that (for unspecified reasons) in "our civilization" "the historian is not so much a collector of facts as a collector and relator of signifiers; that is to say, he organizes them with the purpose of establishing positive meaning and filling the vacuum of the pure series." The "pure unstructured series of notations" (chronologies and annals) are assigned meaning ("signification") by "ideological elaboration, or to put it more precisely, an imaginary elaboration, if we can take the imaginary to be the language through which the utterer of a discourse (a purely linguistic entity) 'fills out' the place of subject of the utterance (a psychological or ideological entity)" (73; 16). It is amusing to observe that the mere mention of "language," albeit metaphorical, drives Barthes inexorably toward a radically constructivist conclusion:

> From the moment that language intervenes (and when would it not intervene?), the fact can only be defined in a tautological fashion. . . . We thus arrive at the paradox which governs the entire question of the distinctiveness of historical discourse (in relation to other types

> of discourse). The fact can only have a linguistic existence (as a term of a discourse), and yet everything proceeds as if this existence were nothing but a pure and simple "copy" of another existence situated in the extrastructural domain, in the "real." This discourse is doubtless the only type in which the referent is aimed for as something external to the discourse, without it ever being possible to attain it outside this discourse. (73; 16–17)

In other words, the discourse of history is caught in a confusion of its own making: mistaking the signified *(signifié)* for the referent.

Historical discourse cannot reach the "real," so it cultivates "the reality effect" *(l'effet de réel)*. It produces this effect by instituting, at least since the nineteenth century, narration as the privileged signifier of the real. The narrative style of history, postulated by Augustin Thierry, "draws its 'truth' from a careful attention to narration, the architecture of articulations and the abundance of expansions (known, in this case, as 'concrete details')" (75; 18).[3] In this, it allies itself with the realistic novel of its time. The "realistic" narrative history closes a paradoxical circle: "Narrative structure, which was originally developed within the cauldron of fiction (in myths and the first epics) becomes at once the sign and the proof of reality" (18).

I have quoted in some detail from the final section of Barthes's essay because it is here that the two-step argument, which is the crux of the postmodern challenge, is developed (and, as far as I can say, has not been noticed until now):

1. Language is incapable of referring to anything outside itself (the world, reality, the past); historiography resorts to narrative in order to make its discourse meaningful and convincing. Narrative replaces, is a substitute for, the "referent," for the "real."

2. History appropriates narrative from fiction, where it was developed and cultivated. Therefore, narrative history is indistinguishable from narrative fiction.[4]

Although Barthes is familiar with contemporary developments and knows that narrative history is not the last word in modern historiography, he maintains that the "relative lack of prominence (if not complete disappearance) of narration in the historical science of the present day"—an obvious allusion to the Annales school—does not disprove but rather confirms his argument: "Historical narration is dying because the sign of History from now on is no longer the real, but the intelligible" (75; 18). In other words, when historiography gives up the ambition to represent the "real" past and is satisfied with making it intelligible, it does not need the crutches of narrative. Is non-narrative history as fictional as narrative history? Barthes does not say. The sentence just quoted is the last sentence of his essay.

The main merit of Barthes's essay is that it injected a truly interdisciplinary thinking into the stale debate about the "rhetoric of history." Hayden White followed in Barthes's tracks when, in his highly influential *Metahistory* (1973),[5] he attempted to construct a "poetics of history," a systematic exploration of the devices of the narrative discourse of history: "I will consider the historical work as what it most manifestly is—that is to say, a verbal structure in the form of narrative prose discourse that purports to be a model, or icon, of past structures and processes in the interest of explaining what they were by representing them" (2). White deserves credit for a logically ordered and forceful formulation of the postmodern challenge. He models historiography as a three-stage activity: first, "the elements in the historical field" (historical events) are arranged sequentially into a chronicle; second, the chronicle is transformed into a story; and third, the story is given a meaning, is "explained," by emplotment. The final step is the most important historiographic operation.[6] Explanation by emplotment is tantamount to encoding the story as a certain "kind of story." Building on Northrop Frye's categories (Frye 1957), White distinguishes four "archetypal" kinds of historical narrative: romance, tragedy, comedy, and satire. Conveniently, the nineteenth-century historians studied by White represent severally the four modes of emplotment: "Michelet casts all of his histories in the Romantic mode, Ranke casts his in the Comic mode, Toqueville used the Tragic mode, and Burckhardt used Satire" (1973, 8).[7]

Proceeding further in Barthes's shadow, White crowns the postmodern theory of history by embedding his narratology in a constructivist philosophy of language. Language operates by and through figuration. All thought, indeed all consciousness, is a tropological "processing of experience" (40). Consequently, the narration of the past is preceded by a hidden "precognitive and precritical" figuration. This stage is a poetic (we should rather say poietic) act in which the historian "both creates his object of analysis and predetermines the modality of the conceptual strategies he will use to explain it" (31). It is, ultimately, the poetics of tropes that "provides us with a basis for classifying the deep structural forms of the historical imagination" (31). Selecting four figures of speech as "mastertropes," White arrives at a second, "deeper" typology of historiography: metaphorical, metonymical, synecdochic, and ironic. Nineteenth-century historiography is seen as moving "from Metaphorical, through Metonymical and Synecdochic comprehensions of the historical world, into an Ironic apprehension of the irreducible relativism of all knowledge" (38).[8]

It is noteworthy that in *Metahistory* White does not equate history and fiction; indeed, as far as I can tell, the term *fiction* does not appear anywhere in the book. White states the equation only in *Tropics of Discourse.* It is instructive to observe how he arrived at it. He repeats that explanation in history is a matching of "a specific plot structure with the set of historical events that he [the historian] wishes to endow with a meaning of a particular kind." But then comes the surprising non sequitur: "This is essentially a literary, that is to say *fiction-making,* operation" (1978, 85, emphasis added). The fatal double equation "emplotment = literary operation = fiction-making" is instituted in the postmodernist paradigm not by analysis but by a substitution of synonyms, or more precisely, by a substitution of terms that White considers to be synonymous. Emplotment is a literary operation; literature is fiction; therefore, history is equivalent to fiction making.[9]

Barthes used the constructivist philosophy of language as the launching pad for the postmodern challenge, whereas for White it was its justification. Later, the double equation "historical narrative = literary narrative = fictional narrative" (often in the simplified form "history equals fiction") became a dogma, repeated without any theoretical justification by a large postmodernist chorus. We can detect slight differences in formulations but no new arguments.[10] It is the *Zeitgeist* that speaks through the chorus.

But I am running ahead of the developments. In the 1970s Hayden White's ideas had barely any impact on the Anglo-American historical profession.[11] Michael Kammen, in his presentation of contemporary

American historical research (Kammen 1980), still ignored the existence of the postmodern challenge. However, that same year a group of historians and philosophers gathered at the Cornell conference that proved to be the beginning of the fast spread of postmodern theorizing in historiography (see LaCapra and Kaplan, eds., 1982). Keith Windschuttle uses the metaphor "deluge" to paint a dramatic picture of this "lethal process" (1996, 7–23). Although Windshuttle laments the storming of "academic strongholds," he himself is evidence that many prominent theorists and prestigious publishing houses did not "surrender." It should not be forgotten that in the middle of the "deluge" Paul Ricoeur explicitly contrasted fiction to historical narrative: "I am reserving the term 'fiction' for those literary creations that do not have historical narrative's ambition to constitute a true narrative." To support the distinction, he recalled the Aristotelian possible, the ancestor of all talk about *possibilia:* "The quasi-past of fiction . . . becomes the detector of possibilities buried in the actual past. What 'might have been'—the possible in Aristotle's terms—includes both the potentialities of the 'real' past and the 'unreal' possibilities of pure fiction" (1984–88, 3:191–92).

Ricoeur was joined in his resistance by at least two other theorists. On the side of the literati, Dorrit Cohn, facing squarely the much-misused case of biography and autobiography, stated firmly: "We cannot conceive of any one given text as more or less fictional, more or less factual, but that we read it in one key or the other—that fiction, in short, is not a matter of degree, but of kind" (1989, 16). C. Behan McCullagh, speaking for the historians, pointed out that "Hayden White and others have performed a great service in exposing the variety of literary and other structures which historians use as frameworks for their accounts of the past. What those philosophers have overlooked, however, is an organizing principle which is peculiar to history and not found in fiction. Historians who write narrative histories generally try to provide a fair overall representation of the central subject of their narrative. . . . In this sense, historical narratives can be true as a whole whereas fictional narratives cannot" (1987, 33).

Every crisis has its beneficial effects. This crisis led to a much-needed debate about the philosophical foundations of historiography. A very powerful response to the postmodern challenge, especially to Hayden

White's claims, came from a group of theorists who devised what I call the "Holocaust test."

## 2. The Holocaust Test

The first to formulate the Holocaust test was Berel Lang, who suggested that the Nazi genocide was a test that should be applied whenever the relationship between fiction and history was argued: "The fact of the Nazi genocide is a crux that separates historical discourse from the process of imaginative representation, perhaps not uniquely, but as certainly as any fact might be required or is able to do" (1990, 158; see also Noiriel 1998, 124). At the time when Lang was writing, Saul Friedlander convened a conference to discuss the test and subsequently published the conference papers (Friedlander, ed., 1992). It is to Hayden White's credit that he agreed to take the Holocaust test. Faced with this traumatic historical event, White splits historical narrative into two levels. The first level is the "account[s] of events already established as facts." On this level, "'competing narratives' can be assessed, criticized, and ranked on the basis of their fidelity to the factual record, their comprehensiveness, and the coherence of whatever arguments they may contain." The second level is constituted by "poetic and rhetorical elements by which what would otherwise be a list of facts is transformed into a story. Among these elements are those generic story patterns we recognize as providing the 'plots.' . . . Here the conflict between 'competing narratives' has less to do with the facts of the matter in question than with the different story-meanings with which the facts can be endowed by emplotment" (1992, 38; see also White 1987, 45).

We might expect White to next deal with the "new," first level of his model, to suggest how in his theoretical framework "events" could become established as "facts" and what the criteria of "fidelity," "comprehensiveness," and "coherence" of competing "historical narratives" would be. Instead, he stays within his old frame of reference and rephrases the test to make it easier: are there any limits on the emplotment, any "unacceptable modes of emplotment" of such periods as the Nazi epoch and of such events as the Final Solution? "We would be eminently justified" in removing the "comic" and the "pastoral" modes from the list of "competing narratives" about the events of the Third Reich.[12] More to the point, characterizing Andreas Hillgruber's controversial emplotment of the defense of the eastern front by the Wehrmacht in the winter of 1944–45 as "tragedy," White for the first time admits that a mode of emplotment can be a distortion rather than an interpretation of history. It is worth our while to quote from this remarkable admission at length:

> Hillgruber's suggestion . . . indicates how the choice of a mode of emplotment can justify certain kinds of events, agents, actions, agencies, and patients that may inhabit a given historical scene or its context. There is no place for any form of low or ignoble life in a tragedy; in tragedies even villains are noble or, rather, villainy can be shown to have its noble incarnations. Asked once why he had not included a treatment of Joan of Arc in his *Waning of the Middle Ages,* Huizinga is said to have replied: "Because I did not want my story to have a heroine." Hillgruber's recommendation to emplot the story of the Wehrmacht's defense of the eastern front as a tragedy indicates that he wants the story told about it to have a hero, to be heroic, and thereby to redeem at least a remnant of the Nazi epoch in the history of Germany. (1992, 43)

In admitting that "in tragedies even villains are noble," White admits indirectly that his "metahistory" fails the Holocaust test. By his way of reasoning, all it would take to make Hitler, Himmler, Heidrich, Eichmann, and others "noble" would be to emplot World War II and the Holocaust as *their* tragedy.[13]

## 3. The House of History Divided

The Holocaust test will impress the practicing historian, but it will not convince a speculative philosopher of history. The latter carries on the postmodern challenge under various labels—"the linguistic turn," "radical constructivism," "deconstructive history." Moreover, it seems that the theoretical awakening of the research historians pushed the late postmodernist to a more radical position. He now pronounces his unsupported dogmas as undisputable truths: "History is first and foremost a literary enterprise." The "disappearance" of history as a sovereign discipline is justified by uncompromising constructivism: "The past is not discovered or found. It is created and represented by the historian as a text, which in turn is consumed by the reader. . . . By exploring how we represent the relationship between ourselves and the past we may see ourselves not as detached observers of the past but . . . [as] participants in its creation" (Munslow 1997, 118, 178). The laborious, often passionate quest to know and understand the past can now be declared to be over, at least by the self-appointed riders of "endism": They "raise for consideration . . . the possibility that not only have we to rethink 'history as we know it' along deconstructionist, postmodern lines, but . . . we may have come to the end of history in all of its current manifestations, that our 'postmodern condition' can perhaps produce its own, nonhistorical acts of the imagination for us to live by which do not figure in their number any sort of recognisable history at all" (Jenkins and Munslow 2004, 2).

Various attempts at a compromise having been unsuccessful, the gap between the postmodern challengers and the defenders of the integrity of history seems to be growing (see *History and Theory* 37 [1998], special issue on Hayden White; and Jenkins, ed., 1997).[14] As is usual in virulent theoretical debates, the original issues have been obscured rather than clarified, and the exchange became more and more repetitive. The furor has become a purely verbal game of interpretations, misinterpretations, interpretations of interpretations, corrections of misinterpretations, and so on.

Despite the radicalization of postmodern "metahistory," the practicing postmodern historians remain moderate (see chapter III). Here let me just quote the great innovator Greg Dening. Although he wants the postmodern historians to adopt the tropes of "the novelists, the painters, the composers, the filmmakers," he refuses to see the past as a mere construct of contemporary imagination: "There is a heavy obligation that I owe the past. If I claim to represent it—if I claim to re-present it—I owe it something, its own independence. I owe it a gift of itself, unique in time and space. The history I write will always be mine and something more than the past, but there is a part of it that is never mine. It is the part that actually happened, independently of my knowing that or how it happened" (2004, 118, 120).

The persistent division within the historical profession and the current radicalization of the postmodern challenge can best be illustrated by the exchange between Perez Zagorin and Keith Jenkins in the journal

*History and Theory* 38 (1999) and 39 (2000). The two discussants differ so in both tone and focus that they tend to speak past each other rather than to each other. Zagorin is concerned primarily with postmodernism's impact on history as a cognitive enterprise, while Jenkins is concerned with the philosophy of postmodernism as a radical "emancipation" discourse.

Zagorin does not see historians split into two radical antagonistic camps, postmodernist and anti-postmodernist. Rather, "there appears to be a wide spectrum of opinions among historians with respect to postmodernism, ranging from substantial agreement and broad endorsement, to noncommittal examination, qualified criticism, and specific reservations, to complete rejection and uncompromising hostility" (1999, 4). He himself offers a defense of the traditional principles of historical research. Remarkably, he calls to assistance the American and British tradition of analytical philosophy, which he sees as a strong alternative to the influence of "Continental" philosophy, on which postmodern philosophy of history primarily relies. He admits that "the interest of analytical philosophers in the philosophy of history has been unduly narrow" but points out that "analytical philosophy's resistance to verbal obfuscation and its insistence on the necessity of clarity and logical correctness seem to me to posit standards of intellectual discourse that are as valid for historians as for philosophers" (5).

The main thrust of Zagorin's criticism is directed against two basic dogmas of the postmodern challenge: the "anti-realist thesis," the claim that "the past is not and cannot be the referent of historical statements and representations"; and the "narrativist thesis," the claim that "the fictional stories invented by writers and the narrations fashioned by historians do not differ from one another in any essential respect" (13, 14).

In his rebuttal of the first thesis Zagorin notes that even those postmodern historians who subscribe to it (such as Elizabeth Ermarth, David Roberts, and Robert F. Berkhofer) cannot avoid making factual statements about the past in their historical texts. Defending the realist position in historiography, Zagorin repeats the simple fact that "to deny the existence of the past as something actual to which historians can refer is . . . futile, because it is an essential condition of the possibility of history as an inquiry" (16). In his rejection of the "narrativist thesis" Zagorin argues that "a historical work differs in essential ways from an invented fiction like the novel, that it doesn't pretend to know or tell everything, and that it is always a selective reconstruction of the past from a great manifold of facts. . . . A history, unlike a novel in the realist genre, consists not only of specimens of narrative but of arguments, footnotes of documentation and justification, acknowledgments of what isn't known, discussions and evaluations of sources and evidence, and critiques of the views of other scholars" (12). Later on in his contribution Zagorin cites a number of significant historical works that "are likely to include pieces of narrative" but are not fundamentally cast in a "narrative mold" and do not really fit "the category of narrative history" (21).[15]

Jenkins's main disagreement with Zagorin's interpretation of postmodern thought concerns its purported anti-realism. Relying heavily on Richard Rorty, Jenkins claims that postmodernists are not anti-realists—that is, they are not denying that "the world is out there"—but "antirepresentationalists." "Antirepresentationalism insists that . . . while our words refer, insofar as they generate meaning, they can only ever refer indirectly—via innumerable mediations—to an actuality that always remains unavailable in its sublimity, its otherness, its radical alterity" (2000, 187). Consequently, "we shall never know what History/history 'really is' (for that will remain secret and undepictable—like the name/face of God)" (193).

It is symptomatic that Jenkins here resorts to what is essentially mystical language, and his idea of transforming postmodernism into "emancipatory discourse" is a mystical vision: "My current argument is that we might now begin to forget historical discourses of the past and begin to live amid the ample and agreeable imaginaries provided by postmodern-type theorists . . . who can generate enough emancipatory rhetorics to eliminate any further kind of foundational or non-foundational past. . . . I think it likely that such new imaginaries—of surprising things to come—may well not include in their number 'histories as we have known them' or, even, histories at all" (200). In Jenkins's version, then, philosophy of history becomes self-destructive: it eliminates the past and its representations from the culture whose advent postmodernism is preparing.

After this, there is no need to dwell on Zagorin's relatively brief "rejoinder," which he wrote, as he says, with "little pleasure" (2000, 201). Perhaps I should just quote his observation about Jenkins's idea of "emancipation," which, as already mentioned, sounds like a mystical vision: "He leaves in obscurity what the emancipation he seeks will consist of and how it will come about. Rather than anything genuine or credible, it resembles a vague, apocalyptic apparition hovering spectrally in the future" (208). In the thinking of Jenkins & Co. postmodernism turns into a quasi-religious utopia in which believers, totally free of the past, will discuss the writings of a few founding fathers and their exegetes and will live without practical concerns, without art, without memory. This postmodernism can contribute nothing to historiography, except to announce its demise.[16]

Most practicing historians saw the postmodern challenge as the latest manifestation of historical relativism. Their response was a restatement of the old argument against historical relativism: "Some claim to 'truth' appears particularly imperative" (Friedlander, ed., 1992, 3). The reassertion of the truth functionality of historical discourse is welcome but does not really meet the postmodern challenge. It leaves intact a claim on which the challenge is based, namely, that there is a necessary and unbridgeable gap between discourse (writing, representation, sign) and reality; no sign, no representation can give us access to reality, can "hook onto reality" (to use Rorty's phrasing). History, being discourse, suffers from the incurable malaise of signs, from their inability to pass from meaning to the world. The paralysis of signification cannot be remedied by a reinterpretation of the concept of discourse; a new understanding of the notion of world is required.

CHAPTER 2

# Representation of the Past and Possible Worlds

THE PRESENT-DAY RESEARCHER is engaged in a desperate struggle with the information explosion. The struggle is especially taxing in interdisciplinary research, where no one can master all the published literature in all the interconnected fields. As interdisciplinary investigations become more and more necessary, they become more and more difficult. An easy way out of this difficulty is to interpret the problems of other disciplines in terms of one's own, a practice typical of quite a few postmodern literary critics. While claiming to cultivate interdisciplinarity, they give philosophy, history, and even natural sciences a "literary" treatment. The concepts popular in postmodern literary criticism, such as subject, discourse, narrative, metaphor, semantic indeterminacy, self-reference, ambiguity, and so on, are applied as a general theoretical framework. Epistemology becomes a clone of literary criticism. This purely verbal reformulation is then hailed as an interdisciplinary triumph of a fashionable critical trend.

Interdisciplinary study governed by the conceptual system of postmodern literary criticism, while posing as a definitive divorce from positivism, presupposes, in fact, the positivistic "territorial principle," that is, the division of cognitive activities into a hierarchy of specialized fields. Yet contemporary cognitive strategies transcend the traditional territorial divisions. While specialized disciplines continue their empirical research, most theoretical advances are achieved in transdisciplinary frameworks, in "hyphenated" sciences, such as psycho-linguistics or bio-chemistry, and in encompassing macrosciences—semiotics, cybernetics, ecological science. Interdisciplinarity is now primarily the formulation of transdisciplinary theories and the positing and testing of higher-order conceptual systems that cut across traditional disciplines. One such cross-disciplinary framework is the conceptual system of possible worlds.[1]

## 1. Possible Worlds

Let us imagine a language that would give us direct access to reality. Every utterance in that language would produce or re-create that portion of the world, that actual object or state of affairs, that the utterance signifies. If by uttering the word *child* you produce and publicly display a child, nobody could deny that your language "hooks onto" reality. Alas, only a divine language, only a magic performative, can produce such special effects.[2] While awaiting a new Prometheus who would steal the divine language for us, we are confined to human language, a language with a weak performative power: it can bring about certain changes in our human affairs, but it cannot create the actual world that exists and goes on independently of language and any other representation. The only worlds that human language is capable of creating or producing are possible worlds. This concept, I believe, is crucial for finding a new response to the postmodern challenge that denies the distinction between historical and fictional representations (see chapter I).[3]

The concept of possible worlds has a venerable philosophical history; today it is commonly associated with the seventeenth-century German rationalist philosopher Gottfried Wilhelm Leibniz. It was resurrected in the 1960s to provide a semantic interpretation of modal logic (Kripke 1963), and then it slowly penetrated the theoretical discourse of natural, social, and human sciences (see Allén, ed., 1989).[4] In the process, the traditional concept had to be adjusted in light of its new tasks.

The first adjustment concerns the origin of possible worlds. In Leibniz's metaphysical conception possible worlds have transcendental existence; they reside in the omniscient divine mind. Contemporary thinking about possible worlds is not metaphysical. Possible worlds do not await discovery in some transcendent depository, they are constructed by the creative activities of human minds and hands. This origin of possible worlds was tersely expressed by Saul Kripke—"Possible worlds are stipulated, not discovered by powerful telescopes" (1980, 44)—and by M. J. Cresswell—"Possible worlds are things we can talk about or imagine, suppose, believe in or wish for" (1988, 4; see also Hintikka 1975,

28; Rescher 1975, 2–3; Adams 1979, 203–5; Bradley and Swartz 1979, 63–64; and Stalnaker 1984, 50–51).

The second adjustment of the concept affects its extent. Possible worlds of logical semantics are "total" or "maximally comprehensive" states of affairs, "maximal cohesive mereological sum(s) of possibilia" (Kripke 1980, 18; Wolterstorff 1980, 131; Yagisawa 1988, 180). Robert M. Adams, following Rudolf Carnap, formulated criteria of "completely determinate" possible worlds: "(1) For every possible world, *w*, and every pair of contradictory propositions, one member of the pair is true in *w* and the other member is false in *w*. (2) Each possible world, if temporally ordered at all, is a complete world history and not a momentary stage of one. The actual world, therefore, includes what has actually existed or happened and what will actually exist or happen, as well as what now exists or happens" (1979, 191; see also Bradley and Swartz 1979, 4–5; and Rescher and Brandom 1980, 2). While the infinite size of complete worlds can be handled by logical formalisms, it is beyond the reach of empirical theories and research methods. Two heuristic moves have been suggested to overcome this problem: *(a)* choose as your universe of discourse a manageable subset of possible worlds that is pertinent to your problem (Hintikka 1975, 75; Kripke 1980, 18); *(b)* design small worlds, "miniworlds," comprising a finite number of elements and determined by a limited number of parameters (Kripke 1980 19; Cresswell 1988, 74; Hintikka 1989, 55; Martin 2005, 96).

Kripke's inconspicuous note is very important because it assures us that the concept of miniworld is logically compatible with the infinite possible world: "If we restrict the worlds to a narrower class of miniworlds, essentially all the issues regarding say, rigid designation, remain the same. So do the questions of modal semantics" (1980, 19n18). The concept of small worlds was taken up and developed by Umberto Eco, who also suggested that outside logical semantics, where possible worlds are "abstract entities like numbers and propositions" (Bradley and Swartz 1979, 63–64), we need "furnished" worlds, possible worlds made up of "individuals endowed with properties" (1989a, 343; 1989b, 55; 1994, 85; see also Coste 1989, 113). Earlier, talking about story worlds, Eco was more specific: "To tell a story you must first of all construct a world, furnished as much as possible, down to the slightest details. If I were to construct a river, I would need two banks; and if on the left bank I put a fisherman, and if I were to give this fisherman a wrathful character and a police record, then I could start writing, translating into words everything that would inevitably happen" (1983, 23). The term *possible worlds* will be used in this book to refer to small worlds comprising particular (concrete) entities.

Possible worlds are not haphazard assemblies of constituents but macrostructures formed by specific global restrictions. These restrictions determine the "general order" of the world, the conditions of existing and acting in that world. A typology of possible worlds is a project in the making, but the basic types are well established. I have in mind the distinction between physically possible and physically impossible worlds. A physically possible world is a world that "has the same natural laws as does the actual world"; in a physically impossible world "the natural laws are different from those in the actual world" (Bradley and Swartz 1979, 6–7; see also Rescher 1975, 144–49).[5] The conditions of existence and acting in a possible world are critically dependent on whether it is a physically possible or physically impossible world.

The idea of possible worlds is a forceful reminder of the contingency of cosmic and human existence. If the basic physical constants were only minutely different, a different universe or no universe would obtain (Rees 1989, 1997). Brutus might not have killed Caesar, Trotsky might have become the leader of the Soviet Union, Nixon could have been a car salesman. Brutus who did not kill Caesar, Trotsky the leader of the Soviet Union, and Nixon the car salesman are possible counterparts of the historical Brutus, Trotsky, and Nixon. The relationship between counterparts, termed *transworld identity,* is formally represented by Jaakko Hintikka's individuation function: it "picks out from several possible worlds a member of their domain as the 'embodiment' of that individual in this possible world or perhaps rather as the role which that individual plays under a given course of events" (1975, 30).[6]

In logical semantics the possible-worlds model does not require ontological commitment. Pointing specifically to Hintikka's and Kripke's proposals, a Russian logician emphasized that they should be taken "simply as mathematical models of the corresponding logical calculi, without any philosophical interpretation" (Slinin 1967, 137). Outside formal logic, however, the notion cannot preserve ontological innocence. As recognized by Robert Adams, it follows the fundamental split in ontology, leading either to actualism or to possibilism. For possibilism, the actual world "does not have a different status" within the set of possible worlds, while for actualism the actual world is "a standpoint outside the system of possible worlds from which judgments of actuality which are not world-relative may be made" (1979, 194, 202; see also Lycan 1979). The actualist position is inscribed in Kripke's original model structure, where set *G* (the actual world) is singled out from the set of sets *K* (all possible worlds) (1963, 804), and is accepted by Plantinga (1974, 45–51), Rescher (1975, 90–92), Stalnaker (1984), Nolt (1986), and Cresswell (1988, 1). In at least one opinion even David Lewis's "indexical" theory (Lewis 1986), which relativizes the concept of actual world, is compatible with "modal realism" (see Miller 1990), that is, with Adams's actualism.[7]

## 2. Fictional and Historical Worlds

The relationships between possible worlds, their similarities and differences, can be seen both in their functions and in their structures. Relocating the problem of the relationship between fiction and history from the level of discourse to the level of world means asking whether the possible worlds of history and fiction are identical in their function and global structure or show some marked differences in these respects.[8] I believe that a number of such differences can be found, but here I shall consider only the most conspicuous ones:

a. *Functional differences.* Fictional worlds are imaginary alternates of the actual world (see Doležel 1998); historical worlds are cognitive models of the actual past.[9] History reconstructs the actual past by constructing models of the past, which have the status of possible worlds. "For me," Braudel writes, "history is the total of all possible histories. . . . The only error, in my view, would be to choose one of these histories to the exclusion of all others. That was, and always will be, the cardinal error of historisizing" (1980, 34).[10] In different branches of history—political, economic, and social history, history of everyday life, history of art, of ideas, of science—possible-worlds models with specific entities are constructed. Thus, the world of political history will be constituted by such semantic entities as national leaders, political figures, political institutions (state, government, parliament, political parties, law courts), political actions (external and internal), political communications and public speeches, political documents (constitutions, laws, international treaties), symbols and emblems (flags, anthems, national colors), and so on.

If representations of the past are seen as partial models of the past in the form of possible worlds, there is no need, no justification, for suppressing historical worlds of a certain semantic character in the name of worlds of a different character. This is a plea for tolerance and synthesis, similar to the one issued by Georg G. Iggers: "There is no reason why a history dealing with broad social transformations and one centering on individual existences cannot coexist and supplement each other. It should be the task of the historian to explore the connections between these two levels of historical experience" (1997, 104).

The postulate of "objectivity" has been a sacred cow of historical theory. The postmodernist thinkers criticized it vigorously. If historical worlds are considered possible reconstructions of the past, then the question of objectivity appears in a different light. Every historical world is a subjective construct, because its author is a person with his or her individual persuasions, scope of knowledge and focus, ideological position, theoretical framework. As a professional, the historian is trained to subordinate personal attitudes to cognitive goals. A historian dealing with the so-called Vichy syndrome maintains: "I have tried within the limits of my power not to become a prisoner of the syndrome I am describing" (Rousso 1995, 648).[11] "Historians," writes Susan Rubin Suleiman, "rely on multiple sources and confront various kinds of documents in constructing their versions of events" (2000, 549). Earlier, Jacques Le Goff quoted with approval Léopold Genicot's distinction between objectivity and impartiality: "Impartiality is deliberate; objectivity is unconscious. The historian does not have the right to pursue a demonstration despite contrary evidence, to defend a cause no matter what it is. He must establish and show the truth of what he believes to be the truth. But it is impossible for him to be objective, to abstract from his ideas about man, and notably when it is a question of gauging the importance of events and their causal relations" (1992, 11–12). Le Goff himself goes one step further. Quoting several historians and philosophers, he aligns himself with the claim that history is a "social practice": "Historiography appears as a series of new readings of the past, full of losses and resurgences, of memory gaps and revisions. . . . An ambitious goal, objective history is slowly constructed little by little, through ceaseless revisions of historical work, the laborious successive rectifications, and the accumulation of partial truths" (110–14). Iggers suggests another way to avoid relativism, even when abandoning "objectivity." Developing the concept of plausibility (see also V.1), he writes: "Plausibility obviously rests not on the arbitrary invention of an historical account but involves rational strategies of determining what in fact is plausible. It assumes that the historical account relates to a historical reality, no matter how complex and indirect the process is by which the historian approximates this reality" (1997, 145). The historical worlds constructed by individual historians enter into a social, increasingly international network of communication, where they are severely tested. The assessment of their adequacy is not a matter of subjective judgment or parochial bias; it is the result of a collective cognitive activity.[12]

b. *Basic structural differences.* The fiction makers are free to call into fictional existence any conceivable world. The borderline between physically possible and physically impossible worlds presents no obstruction to their imagination. They are equally capable of creating physically impossible worlds, called supernatural or fantastic, and physically possible worlds, called natural or realistic, as well as any combination thereof. Every period in literary history has its fantastic and its realistic fiction.[13] In contrast, historical worlds are restricted to the physically possible ones. The boundary between history and mythology lies precisely here. In mythology, supernatural beings (deities, demons, spirits, and so on) are an integral part of the constellation of fictional persons and make their actional contribution to the story. In historical worlds events cannot be assigned to divine agency (even if the historian is a believer). Historical worlds are worlds of natural agents.[14]

When it comes to feats of imagination, nothing is more attractive than impossible worlds. It was Leibniz who circumscribed the universe of the possible by defining the impossible—the worlds that contain or imply logical contradictions. The fiction makers are fascinated by the challenge of constructing impossible worlds, just as mathematicians have been attracted to the impossible task of squaring the circle. In his 1975 book *98.6* Ronald Sukenick constructs an Israel that looks like this: "Here in Israel the extraordinary is run-of-the-mill. We are capable of living in a state in which certain things that have happened have not. At the same time that they have. . . . The way you enter The State of Israel is through Psychosynthesis. In the processes of Psychosynthesis as in the subconscious as in the laws of physics there is no negation." The construction of the impossible world is here displayed as a radical logical rupture, the replacement of standard (classical) logic by nonstandard logic, where "there is no negation."[15] While impossible worlds represent the limit of fiction making, they are unacceptable as historical worlds. Logical contradictions, explicit or implicit, would destroy the structure of the historical world.[16]

c. *Agential constellations.* The cast of agents in the historical world is determined by the set of agents involved in the reconstructed past event(s). If it is revealed, by new documents, say, that a person who did not actually exist or could not have participated in the event was included in a historical world, he or she has to be removed from it. If, on the contrary, new evidence shows that a person who was not included in the historical world participated in the historical event, he or she has to be included in the cast of agents. No such restriction applies to the constellation of agents in fictional worlds. Commonly, this set consists of persons who never existed and are assembled to act and interact by the decision of the fiction maker. This opposition between fictional and historical worlds is clearest when we consider a literary genre in which fiction and history seem to overlap, that is, historical fiction. It is a defining feature of the genre that fictional persons coexist and interact with counterparts of historical persons. Thus, in E. L. Doctorow's *Ragtime* (1974) Emma Goldman, Teddy Roosevelt, Harry Houdini, Sigmund Freud, and others mingle with Father, the little boy, the younger brother, Mameh, Tateh, the little girl, and so on (for details see chapter IV). This feature gives Doctorow's novel its literary effect but invalidates it as a cognitive model of American society at the beginning of the twentieth century. A possible world in which counterparts of historical persons cohabit, interact, and communicate with fictional persons is not a historical world.

Fictional and historical worlds are inhabited, not by real, actual people, but by their possible counterparts. Yet there is a major difference between the fictional and the historical treatment of transworld identity. Fiction makers practice a radically nonessentialist semantics; they can alter all, even the basic, individuating properties of the actual-past persons when transposing them into a fictional world. Verisimilitude is a requirement of a certain poetics of fiction, not a universal principle of fiction making. It is essential for the historical Napoleon that he died at St. Helena. But according to a legend quoted as a motto to Georg Kaiser's play *Napoleon in New Orleans* (1937), Napoleon was rescued from the island and taken to North America and died in New Orleans.[17] The persons of historical worlds (like their events, settings, etc.) bear documented properties. Their physical and mental traits, their temporal and spatial location, their actions and communications are not constructed by free imagination but reconstructed from available evidence. Available evidence, of course, can be richer or poorer, detailed or spotty. Necessarily, the reconstructed historical persons are incomplete, sometimes fragments, often just torsos.

d. *Treatment of incompleteness.* As already mentioned, incompleteness is a general feature of all historical and fictional worlds. It is a necessary feature if we recall that all these worlds are the products of the finite human mind and time. To produce a complete fictional or historical world would require writing a text of infinite length, a task that is beyond human capability. If worlds of fiction and history are incomplete, then gaps are a universal feature of their structure. However, the character, distribution, and treatment of gaps in fiction differ fundamentally from those in history.

The fiction writer is free to vary the number, extent, and functions of the gaps; his choices are determined by aesthetic (stylistic) and semantic factors. For instance, the radically incomplete physique of the romantic hero serves the aesthetic aims of romantic narrative: a physical detail surrounded by emptiness is brought into sharp focus and thus offered for symbolic reading (Doležel 1980). Thomas Pavel, noting that "authors and cultures have the choice to minimize or maximize" the "unavoidable incompleteness" of fictional worlds, has suggested that cultures and periods of a "stable world view" tend to minimize incompleteness, whereas periods of "transition and conflict" tend to maximize it (1986, 108, 109). Marie-Laure Ryan used the degrees of incompleteness as a criterion for a triadic typology of fictional worlds, with realistic fiction striving for the highest degree of completeness but never able to reach it (1984). Lucien Dällenbach came independently to a similar conclusion: the reality-like completeness of realistic narratives is no more than an illusion "destined precisely to camouflage [their] blanks" (1984, 201). What applies to fiction in general applies to historical fiction in particular. The writer of historical novels or stories is free to include in his or her fictional world certain historical facts and omit others. Viktor Shklovsky investigated in detail the choices that Tolstoy made when writing *War and Peace.* Tolstoy omitted well-documented facts that did not suit his aesthetic and ideological purpose.[18]

Since gaps in fictional worlds are created in the act of world making, they are ontic in nature. They are irrecoverable lacunae that cannot be filled by legitimate inference. Statements about fictional gaps are undecidable: to take an example from John Heintz (1979, 94), whether Emma Bovary did or did not have a birthmark on her left shoulder can never be decided. Alluding to a cause célèbre, Nicholas Wolterstorff succinctly explained the ontological character of fictional gaps: "We will never know how many children had Lady Macbeth in the worlds of *Macbeth.* That is not because to know this would require knowledge beyond the capacity of human beings. It is because there is nothing of the sort to know" (1980, 133; see also Rescher and Brandom 1980, 5).[19]

Historical worlds are incomplete in a different manner, and their gaps are of a different kind: they are epistemic, determined by the limitations of human knowledge. Paul Veyne expressed this incompleteness in a grand metaphor: "History is a palace whose full extent we do not discover . . . and of which we do not see all the suites at once" (1984, 261). The first source of gaps is the historian's cognitive strategy, guided either by purely practical considerations (the scope of the investigation) or by a chosen "plot" structure, as Veyne and others would have it. Whatever the motivation, these gaps are a result of the historian's conscious selection,[20] and he or she must be ready to defend it. The other kind of gaps in historical worlds, the gaps that result from lack of evidence, show most clearly their epistemic character: they will be filled if new documents become available. This cognitive progress is a well-known feature of historiography.

Hugh Trevor-Roper's splendid study *A Hidden Life* (1976) is an instructive example of this progress. We are allowed into the historian's workshop and watch him perform two roles: he is simultaneously a detective who uncovers or is given documents about a mysterious person and a writer who constructs a possible life of that person.[21] A major part of Trevor-Roper's detection work is to assess the veracity of the documents attributed to his subject. The historian's razor divides the documents into "reliable evidence" and "fabrication," "fantasy," "fiction," or "forgery." The construction of the historical world can proceed only from reliable evidence. If no such evidence is available, a gap is left in the world, a gap that Trevor-Roper clearly marks as epistemic: "Of Backhouse's duties and success in this post [as professor of law and literature at the University of Peking], which he held for ten years, we know nothing; the documents of the university of Peking have disappeared from human, or at least from Western, sight" (1976, 37). If the documents of the University of Peking are opened for research, then of course this gap in Trevor-Roper's possible life of Edmund Backhouse might be filled.

Absence of documents hampers the historian's reconstruction but does not prevent him or her from hypothesizing. Since the gaps in historical worlds are epistemic, the historian is challenged to "fill" them by plausible conjectures. In reconstructing the past the historian relies as much on inference as on available evidence. The conjectured, hypothesized events are not marked as certain but are assigned a degree of probability. Historians have developed a rich vocabulary of expressions that assess the reliability of their conjectures. Thus Trevor-Roper: *perhaps, it is probable, it is possible, possibly not, conceivably, historically plausible, almost certain(ly), we may surmise, it may well be, we may suspect, we do not know exactly, all this is pure speculation,* and so on. Allan Megill praises Natalie Zemon Davis for following the same strategy in the construction of the historical world of *The Return of Martin Guerre:* she "always clearly identifies her speculations as speculations: 'perhaps' this happened; people 'must have,' or 'would have,' or 'would probably have' done this under this set of circumstances," and so on (2007, 1). The final decision about the factuality of the conjectured events is, so to say, postponed. A critical historian will go no further (see also III.1).

The four distinctions between the properties of fictional worlds and those of historical worlds boil down to an often-stated general contrast between the freedom of the fiction maker and the constraints imposed on the historian. It is the awareness of these constraints that leads scholars to the standard formulation that history is reconstruction of the past. From the viewpoint of possible-worlds semantics, this formulation is unobjectionable as long as we understand that historical reconstruction does not re-create the past in actuality, but in represented possibility.

## 3. Falsified History

Although falsified history is much broader and much more significant, I shall discuss it only in connection with the gaps in historical worlds. We have noted that gaps in historical worlds arise either from a historian's justified selection of represented events or from a lack of supporting evidence. The historian's selection, although unavoidably subjective, is quite different from a deliberate, intentional "gapping" of the past.

Falsified history can occur in any society, but in conditions of a free exchange of ideas it is usually quickly exposed (see, e.g., Vidal-Naquet 2005). In contrast, totalitarian regimes sponsor the creation of a false image of the past to legitimate the current political system, its societal hierarchy, its social representations. Totalitarian-distorted history is the most extreme projection of the interests of the present into the past. Having sponsored the construct, the totalitarian regime enforces it and protects it from falsification by its institutions of oppression, particularly by censorship and by punishment of dissidents. Fortunately, distorted (falsified) history provokes universal aversion. But it is more than a moral issue; it is a theoretically significant abuse of historical representation. It is a sort of laboratory test of the consequences of unbounded historical relativism.

Historical relativism shares with totalitarian history the assumption that representations of the past are always biased by the momentary conditions of their production. Maurice Mandelbaum noticed this feature of historical relativism: "Whatever 'truth' a historical work contains is relative to the conditioning processes under which it arose and can only be understood with reference to these processes." The most prominent among these processes are the historian's personality, the politics of his class and country, and the mental climate of his times (1938, 19). As if following this precept, the historians in the service of totalitarian power studiously apply themselves to a permanent rewriting of history in accordance with the shifting conditions of contemporary politics. The time-serving nature of "directed historiography" is well known. Salo Baron observed that whenever the ruling circles in the Kremlin changed their minds, "certain historical treatments, originally approved by the authorities, were . . . suppressed and replaced by often contradictory evaluations" (1986, 18). The easiest and therefore most popular way to rewrite the past is to erase from historical records and representations the historical figures who have fallen out of favor. A pathetic demonstration of this technique is the deletion of these persons from photographs. Thus Stalin's henchman Yezhov, who was photographed in the company of Stalin and Molotov, disappeared when the picture was remastered after Yezhov fell out of favor and was arrested and shot in 1939. Yezhov evaporated, and nothing of him remains but a small indentation in the wall along which the leaders were walking. A barely noticeable but powerful sign: the past can be gapped by a distorted representation, but somewhere traces remain.

The representations of falsified history might be called fictional except that they are enforced as "true" accounts of the past. Distorted history cannot claim the innocence of fiction. In the conditions of totalitarianism it is not only a rewriting of the past; it is an attempt to remake the past, to create by political power an alternative past. Ultimately, however, the efforts of totalitarian history writers are in vain because the acquisition of historical knowledge proceeds in just the opposite direction: filling in gaps and correcting biases in historical representations. Beyond the reach of totalitarian power, its distorted images of the past are never accepted. And when the power that sustains it crumbles, the distorted images crumble with it and are removed to the trash bin of false representations.

## 4. Worlds and Texts

The postmodern challenge to the distinction between fiction and history was formulated on the level of discourse (texts); I have countered it on the level of possible worlds. Now I shall return to the level of discourse to ask whether the possible-worlds perspective enables us to meet the postmodern challenge on its own grounds. If texts are seen as means of stipulating, projecting, constructing possible worlds, can we formulate some fundamental distinctions between fictional and historical texts?

Possible worlds of fiction are products of *poiesis*. By writing a text the author creates a fictional world that was not available prior to this act. The truth conditions of the fictional text are the key to understanding *poiesis*. As Gottlob Frege recognized, fictional texts (sentences) lack truth value; they are neither true nor false ([1892] 1969, 62).[22] It makes no sense to ask whether Gustave Flaubert was telling the truth or lied when he made Emma Bovary die by poisoning herself. There was no world, no life, no death of Emma prior to Flaubert's writing.

The exemption from truth valuation is only the first step in our conception of *poiesis;* the second, no less important step is the recognition of a specific illocutionary character of fictional texts. Fictional texts are performative: they call possible worlds into fictional existence. The explanation of the world-constructing power of fictional texts is inspired by J. L. Austin's theory of performative speech acts (1962). A possible entity is converted into a fictional existent when it is authenticated by a felicitous, authoritative performative.[23] It is as authenticated possibles that unicorns and fairies, Odysseus and Raskolnikov, Brobdingnag and Chevengur exist, and the reader can gain access to them, fear them, or feel pity for them, talk and argue about them, at any time.

But does the reader's, interpreter's, or literary historian's text share the truth conditions of fictional discourse? Obviously not. It is meaningful, indeed necessary, to ask whether the statement that Emma Bovary died of tuberculosis is true. The sentences about the fictional world of Emma Bovary are constatives in Austin's sense (1971) and as such subject to truth valuation. They are true or false in/of the fictional world that is available as evidence after it has been constructed by the author's writing.[24]

Against this background we can formulate the contrast in the truth conditions of historical and fictional texts. The contrast is grounded in pragmatic conditions, in the functions (aims) of the respective texts (see above, sec. 2). Fictional texts, liberated from truth valuation, construct sovereign fictional worlds that satisfy the human need for imaginative expanse, emotional excitement, and aesthetic pleasure. Historical texts are means of *noesis,* of knowledge acquisition; they construct historical worlds as models of the actual world. Therefore they are constrained by the requirement of truth valuation. Historical text is not performative; it does not create a world that did not exist before the act of representation. Rather, it is constative, a description of a world that preexisted the act of representation. In this respect, historical texts are analogous to texts *about* fictional worlds. Just as it makes sense to ask whether Emma Bovary did or did not commit suicide, so it makes sense to ask whether Napoleon did or did not die on St. Helena. In both cases we talk about truth in/of a possible world, but in the first case the possible world is fictional, whereas in the second case it is a model of the actual past.

This reflection might appear to be just a restatement of the traditional argument against historical relativism (see I.3). But the concept of historical worlds as possible worlds enriches the argument by a crucial lemma: historical texts have to be truth-functional because they stipulate possible worlds that serve as models of the actual past. One and the same historical event, life, or period, for example, can be and has been modeled by diverse historical worlds. The modeling role of possible worlds in cognition has been noted in general terms by Umberto Eco: "We explore the plurality of possibilia to find out a suitable model for realia" (1989b, 57). The nuclear physicist J. S. Bell constructed "six possible worlds of quantum mechanics" as models of the dynamics of elementary quanta. Having presented these possible worlds, Bell poses and answers a question that is crucial for our discussion: "To what extent are these possible worlds fictions? They are like literary fictions in that they are free inventions of the human mind. In theoretical physics sometimes the inventor knows from the beginning that the work is fiction, for example when it deals with a simplified world in which space has only one or two dimensions instead of three. More often it is not known till later, when the hypothesis has proved wrong, that fiction is involved. When being serious, when not exploring deliberately simplified models, the theoretical physicist differs from the novelist in thinking that maybe the story might be true" (1989, 359, 368). Similarly, historians construct the models of the past with the hope that their possible stories "might be true."

In possible-worlds semantics truth valuation does not lead to a final, metaphysical Truth. Its function is pragmatic, one could almost say practical. There is simply no knowledge to be had if we do not postulate the distinction between true and false statements, between genuine artifacts and fakes, between telling the truth and lying, between sincerity and deception. Truth valuation is a never-ending process that demands of historians that they revise continually their historical worlds in order to "supplement or rewrite narratives according to the state of the sources" (Baumgartner 1975, 61). As we learned in section 2 above, history writing is a social cognitive activity. In its critical cauldron historical worlds are permanently tested, modified, confirmed, or rejected.

Our reflection on the distinction between fictional and historical texts is inspired by Frege's philosophy of language. We proceed in the Fregean spirit when we recognize that the different aims of *poiesis* and *noesis* require two different kinds of texts, one performative, with the attending lack of truth valuation, the other constative, with the attending truth functionality. We find ourselves in radical constructivist philosophy when we abolish this distinction and claim that all worlds depend for their existence on texts and that all texts are performative. I do not deny that performative texts create worlds. But these worlds are fictional even though their existence depends on texts that are actual. Performatives, if they are to perform anything, have to originate, have to be uttered in the actual world. Paradoxically, the edifice of constructivist philosophy, on which the equation of fiction and history rests, presupposes the existence of an actual world, because there is no other domicile for languages, representations, words, and texts.

CHAPTER 3

# Postmodern Historical Worlds

*Simon Schama*

THE BIRTH OF MODERN HISTORIOGRAPHY was marked by a shift from the narrative history of the nineteenth-century "classics" to social-science history. This shift is well known and documented (see, e.g., Iggers 1997). Social-science history achieved an unprecedented level of precision and scientific rigor by focusing on social developments, often quantifiable. Emmanuel Le Roy Ladurie apologizes to his readers: "The Carnival [in Romans] and all the elements involved are the point, the plot of my book. . . . I beg indulgence for the flood of statistics in this first chapter. They are not characteristic of the book as a whole but are a necessary part of it, for any history is in part quantitative" (1980, 1). According to Colin Lucas, social-science history brought about a substantial change in the focus of historical representations: "The historian's focus was shifted from the individual to the collective, from political to social history, from description to analysis, from monocausal to multidimensional explanations. . . . The past must be conceived of in terms of structures and systems. . . . Structure in this context does not simply mean social structure, . . . but more importantly the enduring physical, material and eventually mental structures within whose boundaries human individual and collective behavior is confined" (1985, 4–5). However, as usual, the practice does not strictly follow a theoretical precept. Certainly, Le Roy Ladurie, a prominent representative of the social-science history of the Annales school, is not guilty of ignoring the "human factor" of past events; while the tragic events in Romans are played out against the backdrop of economic and social conditions, they are triggered and acted out by individual human agents.

In the postmodern era, a pleiad of prominent historians opened new horizons for historical inquiry, expanding its scope and cultivating new, more reader-friendly styles of presentation. The blossoming has been characterized as an "explosion of historical research into new domains" (Revel and Hunt, eds., 1995, 513); as a manifestation of "history's voracious appetite" to incorporate "new objects," such as "climate, the body, myths, festivals" (Le Goff and Nora 1995, 325); as demonstrating that "the scope of historical writing has expanded enormously in the past thirty years" (Iggers 1997, 7).[1] We witness the emergence of many new "branches" or "modes" of historiography, such as microhistory, the history of everyday life, cultural history, and gender history (see Berenson 1992; Burke, ed., 1992; and Noiriel 1998).[2] Many of these new modes of historiography closely resemble or have even been inspired by literary genres, especially literary biography, the psychological novel, and the postmodern narrative fiction. Again, as in the Romantic era, literature provided templates and means for more personal, more exciting, and more readable representations of the past.[3] A "balancing return" of recent history to the "literary" pole, Noiriel notes, makes historical writing attractive to a nonspecialist readership (1998, 293–94).

But recent historiography did not excommunicate social-science history, nor did it reconfirm the demise of narrative history; it just denied either of them a dominant or exclusive position. The rule of one mode of historiography was replaced by efforts toward a synthesis; a "multifaceted history" appeared on the agenda (Iggers 1997, 103).[4] An example of this synthesis is Edward Berenson's *histoire microscopique* of the trial of Madame Caillaux. His historical world includes not only the trial and its outcome but also "the key ideological and cultural conflicts in which it was embedded." His microhistory is thus able "to illuminate crucial links between gender relations and political conflict, between family drama and high politics, between personal honor and patriotic allegiance" (1992, 8). Our conception of historical worlds as partial models of the past is in full accord with the ideal of "multifaceted history." When partial models are combined and complemented in a tolerant but critical fusion (see II.2), a multifaceted historical representation emerges.

We can state with confidence that in the postmodern period historiography showed remarkable vitality and originality, giving us the fascinating works of Carlo Ginsburg, Lynn Hunt, Jacques Le Goff, Marshall Sahlins, Niall Ferguson, and many others. This boom can be explained by a "natural" evolution of historical research, by its persistent striving to penetrate new domains of the past and include them in the scope of historical representation and by its effort to gain a wider readership. Even Roger Chartier's "methodological changes," particularly his postulate of rethinking "the relation between cultural products and practices . . . and the social world" (1995, 548–49), can be thus explained. This expansion did not require any adjustments in the fundamentals of the philosophy and epistemology of history. We know, however, that at the time when many practicing historians were busy discovering new dimensions of the past, the metahistorians of the postmodern era were questioning the very foundations of historical research (see chapter I). I formulated a theoretical response to the postmodern challenge in chapter II. In this chapter I demonstrate how this challenge affected practicing historians. Is there a postmodern historiography? And if there is, what kind of historical worlds does it construct?

## 1. Postmodern Historians

As already mentioned, most of the historians who were engaged in expanding the scope and diversity of historical worlds did not cultivate historiography according to the postmodern creed. Referring to Peter Burke's anthology (1992), Robert F. Berkhofer Jr. writes (or complains): "Most [essays] show that advocating a broadened approach to what history should include as areas of interest need not lead to any fundamentally new forms of historical representation of their entities as subjects or in their textualization as context" (1997, 278–79). Berkhofer pointed out that only some new areas of history tend to show an inclination to postmodern experimentation, particularly histories of historical representations, local histories, and ethnohistories (264, 365n71, 279). It is important for our purpose to record that Berkhofer singles out a few titles that meet many of his criteria for the "new textualization" of the past, among them primarily Greg Dening's *Mr. Bligh's Bad Language: Passion, Power and Theater on the Bounty* (1992), Richard Price's *Alabi's World* (1990), Robert Rosenstone's *Mirror in the Shrine: American Encounters with Meiji Japan* (1988), and Simon Schama's recent books, especially *Citizens: A Chronicle of the French Revolution* (1989).

It should not escape our attention that Berkhofer's selection procedure is typical of traditional literary critics. He first formulates a conception of the new historical "textualization" and then turns it into criteria of a normative (prescriptive) poetics. Some of these postulates are rather difficult to satisfy:

> A new contextualization must combine multiple contexts with novel ways of contextualizing them through their representations. It must combine metahistory and history, Great Stories and historiography while historicizing itself as it historicizes its subject matter; the postulated evidential past and the multifarious present should create each other as they problematize each other. It must combine discourses and counterdiscourses about poetics and politics, texts and textualization, and the other dilemmas historicization tries to resolve as it embodies them. It must theorize about what it theorizes as it theorizes and exemplify its models as explicitly as possible. Such textualization deconstructs itself as it (re)constructs history through its representation. (275)

After contemplating this "recipe," one is tempted to agree with the impressive trio of critics of postmodern metahistory Joyce Appleby, Lynn Hunt, and Margaret Jacob, who assume that "in the final analysis . . . there can be no postmodern history" (1994, 237). This position would end any further search, but that would be premature. Let us not give up hope. We are encouraged by Allan Megill, who can think of "a small body of stylistically 'experimental' works of history," giving as examples Jonathan D. Spence's *Death of Woman Wang* (1978), Natalie Zemon Davis's *Return of Martin Guerre* (1983) and *Fiction in the Archives: Pardon Tales and Their Tellers in Sixteenth-Century France* (1987), Robert Rosenstone's *Mirror in the Shrine,* and David Farber's *Chicago '68* (1988) (1995, 171, 271n83). A confusing maneuver comes from an anthology compiled by Keith Jenkins under the misleading title *The Postmodern History Reader:* "This *Reader,*" he states, "is primarily on postmodern-type theories of historiography: on 'the nature of historiography' under the impact of the 'posts.' But questions which often arise in this context are what, after all this theorizing, do (or would) postmodern histories actually look like?" Jenkins provides several answers to this question, all of them quite unsatisfactory. First he claims that postmodern histories "are 'histories of the future,' histories 'which have not yet been.'" Then, however, he discovers "intimations of postmodern-type histories" in the works of Hayden White, Jean Baudrillard, Natalie Zemon Davis, Simon Schama, Stephen Bann, and others. Jenkins also refers to some works in Berkhofer's selection, the books by Greg Dening, Richard Price (whose title he gives as *Alibi's World*), and Robert Rosenstone. Finally, Jenkins directs his readers to Ankersmit and Kellner's anthology *A New Philosophy of History* (Jenkins 1997, 28). Why a reader should find works of history in that volume is not explained. And indeed, the reader finds none, despite Jenkins's recommendation. Our last list, Iggers's, is rather short. He suggests that "perhaps Simon Schama's *Dead Certainties: Unwarranted Speculations* (1991) and Jonathan Spence's *The Question of Hu* (1987) went farthest in the direction of a historiography that consciously dissolved the border between scholarly history and historical novel" (1997, 135). But this suggestion is spurious, at least with respect to Schama's work. Schama did only one thing "consciously": he declared *Dead Certainties* a work of fiction (see below, sec. 3.3).

Berkhofer shows that a radical, vocal, but relatively uninspiring trend has taken over the postmodern thinking about how to write history. Alun Munslow, the most dogmatic of the propagandists of the deconstruction of history, writes: "The genuine nature of history can be understood only when it is viewed not solely and simply as an objectivized empiricist enterprise, but as the creation and eventual imposition by historians of a particular narrative form on the past" (1997, 2).

Obviously, White's original contention that there is no fundamental distinction between historical and fictional narrative has been radicalized: Historiography does not re-present the past; it creates it. Moreover, contemporary historiography can no longer be satisfied with following the model of the realistic narrative, characteristic of nineteenth-century fiction. Echoing Hayden White's complaint, Robert Rosenstone encourages contemporary historians "to write History that incorporates the techniques or strategies of twentieth-century literature" (2004, 4).[5] He himself has provided an example in his *Mirror in the Shrine*.

## 2. Replacing Historical by Fictional Worlds

Why would a historian resort to "techniques or strategies" of modern fictional narrative? In Rosenstone's case, because he is dissatisfied with traditional historical modes of representation: "When I began to write

[*Mirror in the Shrine*], it was in the same, third-person style that I had used in two previous books. But after producing some two hundred pages, I realized that this traditional form was not working for me. Was not satisfying me. What do I mean? Somehow the writing did not convey what I wanted to say about the past. Did not let me get close enough to my characters. Did not let me see the world through their eyes, smell it through their noses" (3). The historian disposes of the traditional historical narrative because he sets himself tasks that it cannot fulfill. Only fictional narrative can achieve what Rosenstone "wanted to say about the past," re-creating intimate experiences of unique historical characters.[6]

Rosenstone does not designate his experimental representation of the past as fiction. He insists that the experimental historians have not given up "on historical knowing. They simply realize that such knowledge must sometimes be expressed in new ways" (2). But some of the experimental historians represented in Munslow and Rosenstone's *Experiments in Rethinking History* (2004) give up the pretense and freely invent fictions about the past when they are frustrated as historians.[7] Bryan Simon pursues more consistently than Rosenstone the postmodern historian's "progress," creating the past by replacing historic reconstruction with fictional construction. Simon "advances" in three steps.

*Step 1.* For the first version of Simon's story we have to look to his book *A Fabric of Defeat: The Politics of South Carolina Millhands, 1910–1948* (1998). This is a traditional labor history of South Carolina millworkers, focusing not only on their work and living conditions but also on their political and racial ideology. It opens with the story of the white millworker Joe Childers, who met two young African Americans near the train station in the small town Blacksburg. The historian comments: "What happened that night among Childers, Brinson, and Whisonant will never be known. Depending on who told the story, Childers either asked Brinson and Whisonant to get him a pint—or a quart—of whiskey or the two African Americans badgered the innocent man until he finally agreed to buy liquor from them. The three men got drunk" (11). Childers later appeared at the police station and accused the two African Americans of sexual assault. The next morning they were arrested, found guilty, and fined twenty dollars each. Because they had no money, they were placed in the local jail. During the night the prison was broken into and Brinson and Whisonant were lynched "by persons unknown." Two major gaps exist in this historical world: what happened between Childers and the African Americans after they got drunk and the lynchers' raid on the prison. Both episodes are covered by the darkness of night.

*Step 2.* Simon's 2004 essay "Narrating a Southern Tragedy: Historical Facts and Historical Fictions" is divided into two unequal parts. In the short first part, entitled "Historical Fact," the historian reprints the available contemporary documents about the Blacksburg lynching. This is the part of the story that we "know." Unfortunately, none of the reprinted documents—newspaper reports, a letter from a lawyer to the governor of the province, and census data—help to fill in the historical world's gaps.

*Step 3.* The frustrated historian decides to fill in the gaps by writing fiction. He confesses: "I was tempted by fiction. I say this with a certain amount of guilt and shame. I was tempted by the freedom and imagination of fiction; I was tempted by how fiction gave me the chance to wander through the heads of my historical characters, I was tempted by the simultaneous ambiguity and certainty of fiction; and finally, I was tempted by the interior perspective of fiction—an interior perspective of people's private thoughts and anxieties that historians rarely explore in print because the evidence rarely gives us access to these worlds. In the end, I was tempted to say what I really thought was happening" (1998, 182). Indeed, the ultimate aim of this fiction is to tell a "true" story. The only way to do this is to write a mimetic story, using universalist mimesis, usually a tool of interpretation, as a tool for creating a story.[8] Simon's historical fiction is not a product of creative imagination; it is an exemplum of the state of the society and social relations in the mill country of South Carolina at the beginning of the twentieth century.

But what do we learn about the past when we fill in the gaps in the historical world by fictional invention? I am afraid that the cognitive gain is nil, for two reasons. First, Simon's historical fiction gives us two versions of "what might have happened." One story tells of the African Americans committing a "fearful crime," the other about Childers's provocation and guilt. But this ambiguity was evident to us after the first step of Simon's investigation. The second, theoretical reason is more significant: knowledge provided by fiction is fundamentally different from knowledge provided by historical inquiry. Historical knowledge is a reconstruction of the past produced by research. It is truth-functional and therefore constantly revised in the critical social practice of falsification and/or verification. Fictional knowledge, even if it is based on historical research, is constructed by imagination and therefore is beyond truth valuation. We can agree or disagree with fictional knowledge, but it cannot be independently falsified or verified (see II.4). Some postmodern historians obviously like to wear two hats, that of historian and that of fiction writer. A young historian who found sketchy evidence of the lynching of two young African Americans in 1912 and wants to get at the "full" story at any price writes a fictional narrative, believing that it is "a way to explore the past," not "a way to distort or misrepresent" it (Simon 2004, 180–81).

In Simon we rediscover a historian who—like Walter Scott and his nineteenth-century followers—uses historical inquiry and its results to write historical fiction. There is nothing postmodern nor experimental about the "temptation" to do this. Just like his classical predecessors, Simon finds in fiction what he lacks in history. This is not a new conception of history nor a new representation of the past. It is simply a rejection of historical representation in favor of fictional narrative. If all young historians turn into historical-fiction writers, the postmodern philosophy of history has failed in its effort to "teach" historians how to write new history.

If fiction making is not a way toward postmodern historiography, what is? I suggest that the features and qualities of postmodern historiography are nowhere more apparent than in the writings of Simon Schama. I shall try to provide answers to the questions posed at the beginning of this chapter by studying meticulously his remarkable and varied *oeuvre.*

## 3. Simon Schama

Schama's archival research and his study of secondary literature cover almost all contemporary modes of historiography. His striving for synthesis leads to the creation of complex and comprehensive historical worlds. His style has absorbed features of the literary and essayistic verbal art and appeals to a wide readership. But there is more to his accomplishment. He is, first of all, a historian who demonstrates and proves that postmodern historiography did not jettison the virtues that ensure the integrity of historical research.[9]

### 3.1. NARRATING THE PAST: *CITIZENS: A CHRONICLE OF THE FRENCH REVOLUTION*

To my knowledge, Schama has not spelled out systematically his views on the nature, purpose, and method of historical inquiry. He deliberates on these matters and formulates a coherent stance in the prefaces and introductions to his books and in numerous statements dispersed throughout his works. His comments in the preface and prologue of *Citizens* contribute to this explicit theory of historiography. Schama plunges into the center of postmodern controversies about writing history and responds to the radical skepticism of the postmodern challenge. Having stated that he reconstructs the French Revolution "in the form of a narrative,"[10] he naturally considers Hayden White's argumentation: "Narratives have been described, by Hayden White among others, as a kind of fictional device used by the historian to impose a reassuring order on randomly arriving bits of information about the dead." Conceding that "there is a certain truth to this alarming insight," Schama avoids a direct confrontation with the metahistorian by aligning himself with another theorist: "My own point of departure was provided by a richly suggestive article by David Carr in *History and Theory* (1986) in which he argued a quite different and ingenious case for the validity of the narrative" (1989, xv–xvi). In the article Carr proposes that "narrative activity . . . is practical before it becomes cognitive or aesthetic in history and fiction" (1986a, 126). The article is just a brief abstract of his book *Time, Narrative, and History*. Drawing on the phenomenology of time and action, he argues against those "narrativists" who claim that "ordinary experience, unnarrated, consists of 'mere sequence'" and points out that "events combine to make up larger-scale events of which they become structural, not merely sequential, elements" (1986b, 52). "Narrative is not in any way adventitious or external to the actions and experiences of real life but a part of its fabric. . . . Insofar as [historical] inquiry results in narrative accounts, these must be regarded not as a departure from the structure of the reality they purport to depict, much less a distortion or radical transformation of its character, but as an extension of its very nature" (52, 168, 169).[11]

*Citizens* is a contribution to the debate about history and fiction not in the formulation of another "metahistory" but in the practice of a new historiography: “What follows (I need hardly say) is not science,” writes Schama. “It has no pretensions to dispassion. Though in no sense fiction (for there is no deliberate invention), it may well strike the reader as story rather than history. It is an exercise in animated description, a negotiation with a two-hundred-year memory without any pretence of definitive closure” (6). Neither narrative (story) nor “animated description” necessarily produces fiction. While both require a mobilization of literary, rhetorical, and narrative devices, they do not affect the truth-functional status of historical discourse. Schama’s is a nonfiction story.[12] Even the most private experiences of historical persons and the most incredible adventure stories (such as the Diamond Necklace Affair) are supported by meticulous documentation in the text itself or in the bibliography.[13]

Schama’s “narrative history” of the French Revolution is an alternative to the favored twentieth-century picture of the earth-shattering event: a major political change determined by changes in economic and social structures. In Schama’s view, the social-science-oriented history does not adequately explain this historical upheaval. The Revolution does not conform “to a grand historical design, preordained by inexorable forces of social change. Instead it seems a thing of contingencies and unforeseen consequences. . . . As the imperatives of ‘structure’ have weakened, those of individual agency, and especially of revolutionary utterance, have become correspondingly more important” (1989, xiv; see also Burke 1992a, 236).

Like all other historical worlds, the world of *Citizens* is full of gaps. The gaps in documentation are meticulously noted and, just as in Trevor-Roper’s historical biography (II.2), filled by conjecture. Schama’s text is full of probability operators: *undoubtedly* (21), *possibly* (22), *perhaps* (24, 518, 665), *more likely* (52), *probably true* (98), *no doubt* (346), *it seems* (377), *it is hard to know* (538), *we do not know* (599), *likely* (681), and *almost certainly* (683), among others. A very telling example of this device occurs in the description of the aftermath of the king’s execution. Commenting on a passage from the memoir of a witness, the historian suggests that “much of his account is likely to have been true. Sanson [the executioner] was entitled to sell items of clothing and mementoes from the execution as part of his perquisites. Less reliably documented . . . are accounts of spectators saturating their handkerchiefs in the royal blood" (670–71). As stated in II.2, the conjectures represent a "gray" area in the historical world, an area of virtual historical facts that await their confirmation or dismissal by further research and documentation.

Schama practices multiperspectival history by creating a multilayered historical world of a particular semantic structure. Political social acting inevitably dominates the world of a revolution.[14] But in Schama's world the agents of this acting, all counterparts of historically attested persons, are not anonymous enforcers or destroyers of social structures; they are individuals with particular personality traits, attitudes, beliefs, talents, and private lives. This historiography, as Iggers pointed out, "wishes to rescue the unknown [individual] from oblivion." Therefore, "a new conceptual and methodological approach to history is called for that sees history no longer as a unified process, a grand narrative in which the many individuals are submerged, but as a multifaceted flow with many individual centers. Not history but histories, or, better, stories, are what matter now. And if we are dealing with the individual lives of the many, we need an epistemology geared to the experiences of these many that permits knowledge of the concrete rather than the abstract" (1997, 103).[15]

In political history (including its military branch) individuals necessarily become roles in more or less tightly organized groups. Yet in Schama's world, even the formally organized groups, the institutions, are not intentionless automata; the historical persons' distinctive performance of their institutional roles influences the functioning of the institution. A major strain of Schama's story is the struggle for the control of political institutions of the French state. His model allows him to represent this struggle not only as a replacement of certain political institutions by others but also as a transformation of political institutions by the replacement of the acting teams. But a historical world of a revolutionary period would be woefully inadequate if it did not include unorganized groups—crowds or mobs. They complete the assembly of Schama's historical agents, a complex web of individuals, organized social groups, and mobs. This cast performs the drama of the Revolution, which is ultimately dominated by the struggle between the power of revolutionary institutions and the elementary power of the capricious mob.[16]

At the very beginning of his world construction Schama demonstrates his method of creating the individual agents of the French Revolution, the Patriots. He sets up a major "symbiotic" contrast between two of the principals, Talleyrand and Lafayette. This contrast is defined in the "postfestum" prologue, where Schama takes a snapshot of the two men during the revolution of 1830: "In their own persons, Lafayette and Talleyrand embodied the split personality of the French Revolution. For while it is commonplace to recognize that the Revolution gave birth to a new kind of political world, it is less often understood that that world was the product of two irreconcilable interests—the creation of a potent state and the creation of a community of free citizens" (1989, 15). Returning to their youth in the first chapter, Schama complements the contrast by a similarity: both young men found and followed a spiritual "father"—Talleyrand, Voltaire; and Lafayette, Washington. The biography of these "new men," who acted out a major historical rupture, also demonstrates the continuity of history.

Schama's narrative "weaves" the biography of the revolutionary leaders "between the private and public lives" because they "saw their own lives as a seamless whole, their calendar of birth, love, ambition and death imprinted on the almanac of great events" (xvi). Talleyrand, who grew from "a worldly young cleric" into an elegant diplomat, is a passionate lover of women with "a long line of amours" (22). The gallery of Talleyrand's mistresses is contrasted with Lafayette's lifelong love for his wife Adrienne (whom he married at the age of fourteen) and his devotion to their children. Adrienne was at his side not only in his triumphs but also during his most cruel deprivation, in the Olomouc prison. An examination of Robespierre's private life, however briefly represented, adds a conspicuous and unforgettable trait to the character of the Incorruptible: "His domestic arrangements were well known and advertised as exemplary. From mid-1791 he lodged with the family of the Duplays in the rue Saint-Honoré. Duplay was a carpenter and cabinet maker. . . . Settled in a small room with writing desk and chair, Maximilien Robespierre emerged in the evenings to take a simple meal and read to the Duplay girls Corneille or Rousseau while peeling the oranges of which he was inordinately fond" (579).

The world of *Citizens* is inhabited by a host of secondary agents and episodic characters who are individualized by summarized life histories. The formation of the Patriot is presented not only in the *Bildungs*-story of Talleyrand and Lafayette but also in stories of many other revolutionaries, among them Lally-Tolendal. The young orphan "was set on course to become a revolutionary aristocrat by his crusade to vindicate the reputation of his father [the biological father this time], who had been tried and executed as a scapegoat for French military failure in India." When, after much effort, the father is vindicated, Lally-Tolendal sets out on the same pilgrimage that Talleyrand made: he visits Voltaire, who, "on his deathbed, placed his hands on the head of the young noble as a last act of paternal blessing" (31, 32). We should not be surprised that Schama, the art historian, draws into the historical world visual emblems (such as narrative paintings of Bellisarius and *The Oath of the Horatii*) as well as literary images of patriotic heroes of the Roman Republic and French history.[17] This is an indication of the major role of semiotic objects in Schama's world.

I have stated that Schama builds his historical world in contrast to the world of social history. At the same time, in an adequate model of a revolution major economic and social forces have to have a prominent place in the historical world. The heavy burden of the French support of the American Revolution and the efforts of Louis XVI administration to rebuild the French navy are blamed for the rising debt of the French treasury. But even in the reconstruction of these social events Schama does not pass over the contribution of individuals. France gets involved in American affairs only after a fierce struggle between the finance minister, Turgot, and the foreign minister, Vergennes (48). On the other hand, a personal trait, if it is the king's, can turn into a major policy initiative: Louis XVI, who as a boy "had played with toy galleons and barques," "became a passionate and compendiously knowledgeable expert on everything naval" (55). When king's passion becomes state policy, no expenditure is big enough to transform France into a major naval power.

As Schama's narrative proceeds toward the gigantic confrontation, the social domain of the historical world assumes greater and greater importance. We get a detailed reconstruction of the "farmers" *(fermiers)* system of indirect tax collection (ch. 1), of the conflicts between the crown and the parliaments (ch. 3), of the boom in the mass media (ch. 4), and of the economic growth in the last years of the *ancien régime* (ch. 5). As the Revolution progresses, the "heroes," with their colorful characters and exciting life stories, are increasingly overshadowed by the faceless masses as agents of social action.[18]

The institutional stratum of Schama's historical world is dominated by the National Assembly in its several embodiments—the Estates General, the National Constituent Assembly, the Legislative Assembly, and the Convention. Schama reconstructs in detail the turbulent story of the legislative power that transformed France. While there is practically no mention of the deliberations and decisions of the various governments of the day or of the royal council (which was convened up to the end of the monarchy), the membership of the National Assembly, its leaders and factions and particularly its great orators, is central to Schama's narrative. The power of the Revolution emanated from the power of "the voice," from the rhetorical fireworks that make the sessions of the National Assembly a special chapter in the history of political oratory. From Mirabeau's powerful speeches, "not so much written as uttered" (344), to the fierce maiden speech of Saint-Just in the Convention, the Revolution becomes a tournament of eloquent rhetorical performances that first determine the fate of the *patrie* and then decide about the life or death of the Patriots.

The relationship between the leaders and the masses changes dramatically as the Revolution progresses. In the first phase, the leader's "voice" excites the masses to action, but soon the mass action takes a course of its own, no longer controlled. The so-called Day of Tiles in Grenoble (the veritable beginning of the Revolution, on June 7, 1788) starts with the clerks of the parliament "haranguing people in the markets and distributing pamphlets and posters. . . . The protest moved from speeches, shouted insults and songs to a strike" (274). Ultimately, in the confrontation with soldiers "many of the Grenoblois took to the roofs of their houses and began pelting the unprotected soldiers with tiles until a rain of them was clattering onto the cobbles below" (275). The decisive events of July 1789 were actually launched on July 12 by an impassioned speech of the brilliant twenty-six-year-old orator Camille Desmoulins in the favorite gathering place of the Parisians, the Palais Royal. "The audience response was gratifying. Desmoulin was an instantaneous hero, surrounded by arms clasping him, shouts of 'bravo,' kisses, fiery oaths never to abandon his side" (382). From there on, however, unorganized masses took the matter into their own hands. They forced the withdrawal of royal troops from Paris, seized a quantity of weapons, and on July 14 took the Bastille. It is interesting that there were no eloquent speeches before the battle, just shouts of "Give us the Bastille!" from the crowd (402). But even in this mass action some individuals can be identified and given the honorary title *vainqueur* (see esp. 402).

Ultimately, the leaders lost control of the masses. No one was faced with the dilemma "of how to remain the master, rather than the helpless servant, of revolutionary force" more critically than the commander of the National Guard, Lafayette, who "was confronted daily by desperately hungry, irrational, suspicious crowds that could turn within hours from anger to murder. Lafayette had to develop, very rapidly, skills as labor negotiator, arbitrator, militia commander and political diplomat. The wonder is not that his powers were eventually to fail him but that he managed to exert control in the capital for as long as he did" (449). The crowds are now called into action by the tocsin and by their own shouts rather than by the eloquent speeches of the Patriots. The march of the Parisian women to Versailles on October 5, 1789, was triggered by an anonymous "market woman" who harangued the crowd, "blamed the Queen for their starvation and urged her listeners to march on Versailles to demand bread" (460). There were no speeches before the bloody attack of August 10, 1792, on the Tuileries—we glimpse Desmoulins "set[ting] off into the night, carrying a musket" (613)—which marks the end of the monarchy, nor before the "holocaust" of the September prison massacres. In the final stage of the Revolution even the masses become silent and passive, spectators of the daily travails of the guillotine. There are no crowds defending Robespierre and his Jacobin friends.

The Revolution leads to an end state that is very similar to its initial state: the masses under the dictatorial power of the state: "The institutional machinery for the revolutionary dictatorship . . . was now set in place, so that the chaotic brutalities of the street mobs would be replaced by the systematic machinery of state punishment" (731).[19] The establishment of the state dictatorship means the ultimate failure of the Revolution: "The Terror thus represented the liquidation of the original dream of the Revolution: that liberty and patriotic power were not only reconcilable but mutually dependent. Accordingly, what seemed the most irrepressible feature of the French Revolution—its political effervescence—was trapped inside the bottle of a national dictatorship. Politics had to end so that patriotism might conquer: that would be the founding creed of Bonapartism" (755).

A conspicuous device of the individualization of narrative is Schama's introduction of exact time and space indices of events and actions. This device is especially effective at the beginning of chapters or sections of narrative: "On a warm morning in 1783, in the Atlantic harbor of Brest, René de Chateaubriand had a vision" (60); "One morning in August 1776, a rather shabbily dressed, stout gentleman [Malherbes] stood at the dockside at Rotterdam" (96); "On September 19, 1783, at around one in the afternoon, to the sound of a drum roll, an enormous taffeta spheroid [the Montgolfiers' balloon] wobbled its way unsteadily into the sky over the royal palace at Versailles" (123); "On July 13, 1788, a hailstorm burst over a great part of central France from Rouen in Normandy as far south as Toulouse" (305); "The little grain market town of Machecoul lay twelve miles from the Atlantic. Just after dawn, on the eleventh of March 1793, seven-year-old Germain Bethuis was woken by a dull, booming noise rather like the sound of an angry sea" (690; documentation of Bethuis's account of the massacre at Machecoul, the beginning of the Vendée, is given on 900); "On a crisp late September day in 1794, in the Hudson Valley, a young woman [Mme de La Tour du Pin] sat outside her log house boning a leg of lamb" (861; see her Journal, cited on 905).

Schama's mode of historical writing is unorthodox compared with its immediate predecessor, social-science history, but it is not unprecedented in the history of historiography. Indeed, its link to Romanticism becomes quite obvious when we consider its main qualities. According to Harry Elmer Barnes, Romantic historiography was characterized by three features: "One was the Romanticist theory that history should be vivid and interesting, and hence, that the finest sort of historical material was to be discovered in dramatic episodes. The other was the view, drawn largely from Carlyle and his disciples, that history is collective biography. Hence, the personal element loomed large in this variety of historiography." Finally, "Romanticism served to broaden the ken of the historian by interesting him in religion as a universal institution, as well as in philosophy, art, and letters" (1962, 293, 294).

Also in the Romantic spirit, the postmodern historian does not hide his subjectivity. But as demonstrated by Philippe Carrard, already in the Annales school texts, despite theoretical pronouncements to the contrary, "the overt presence of the enunciator" is a "recurrent feature," evident in the numerous instances of the first-person narrative, in the subjectivization of commentary, and in the presentation of the historian as histor. The Annales historians "take sides, not only commenting upon their material in an academic manner . . . , but actually expressing strong individual beliefs, feelings and opinions. . . . They . . . may express personal opinion with . . . brutal directness, particularly when they comment on what they deem to be acts of violence or injustice against the oppressed" (1995, 112–16). In Schama's *Citizens, Ich*-form utterances occasionally give a personal flavor to the orthodox *Er*-form of historical narrative: "I do not want to minimize the impact of the early Revolution on French life and institutions" (1989, 518). "I have quoted Vergniaud at length because his speech represents a rare attempt to stay back from the fray and survey the revolutionary landscape" (715). More fundamental features of subjectivity are the historian's explicitly or implicitly stated attitudes, especially irony and anger. The book is full of ironies (a favorite figure of the postmodernist), usually triggered by surprising, dramatic turns of events or personal fortunes, which of course happened too often during a revolutionary period. Of Versailles after the king and his family were taken to Paris on October 6, 1789, he writes: "Supervised by M. de La Tour du Pin, the great palace of Louis XIV was being boarded up. . . . Le Brun's Apollo king still rode his chariot against the upstart Dutch on the ceiling of the empty Hall of Mirrors, but the walls of the marble staircase were pockmarked with shot. Versailles had already become a museum" (470). On the king before the execution, he writes: "When representatives from the Commune arrived, he asked them if Cléry might not cut his hair to spare him the indignity of being cropped on the scaffold. Needless to say, permission was denied. He was, for the purposes of the executioner, just another head" (668). Often, the event itself is so absurd that it is implicitly ironic: When the "first martyr of the revolution," the Jacobin deputy Michel Lepeletier, was murdered, his daughter "was declared to be 'adopted by the nation,' though she scarcely had then need . . . since her father's legacy came to some half-million livres. Later, this *fille de la nation* would become a passionate royalist" (673).

Schama's ironic attitude is all-pervasive, his irony directed at human folly and the folly of human history. The more violent the means of the revolution, the less they can assure its utopian goals. Humans cannot be forced into utopia, however attractive it might be. Ultimately, the goal of the revolution will collide with the realities of the political and economic situation, and the revolution will abandon all its ideals and replace them with *Machtpolitik*. This kind of irony is not an expression of a conservative attitude toward the Revolution; it is a disappointed liberal's doubt that the human race could arrange its social and political affairs in an optimal or at least beneficial manner.

Schama's anger is directed primarily at the cult of violence that the Revolution proclaimed and cultivated from the beginning: "From the very beginning—from the summer of 1789—violence was the motor of the Revolution. . . . While it would be grotesque to implicate the generation of 1789 in the kind of hideous atrocities perpetrated under the Terror, it would be equally naïve not to recognize that the former made the latter possible. . . . All these features of what historians have come to designate the 'political culture of the Revolution'—were the products of the same morbid preoccupation with the just massacre and the heroic death" (859). In a polemic against "the scholarly normalization of evil," Schama spells out his principle: "To those who insist that to prosecute is not the historian's job, one may reply that neither is selective forgetfulness practiced in the interest of scholarly decorum" (632). The postmodern historian remembers the horrors of mass killings perpetrated by perverse political regimes of the twentieth century; therefore he cannot forget the horrors of the years 1792–94: "Caron was writing . . . in 1935. Ten years later, European history was again disabused of the notion that modernity somehow confers exemption from bestiality" (636). In his mention of the French historian Pierre Caron, Schama alludes to Caron's book on the September 1792 prison massacres, which he calls "a monument of intellectual cowardice and moral self-delusion. . . . Caron argued that the massacres were, somehow, no one's responsibility. Rather, they were the inevitable product of impersonal historical forces. . . . The overall effect is meant to be comforting for the revolutionary historian: the scholarly normalization of evil" (631). Schama will never engage in this "scholarly normalization of evil." On the contrary, he points his finger at those who were responsible, from Roland and Danton, members of the government who did nothing to prevent or stop the massacres, through the "commissaires" Maillard and Ceyrat, who passed the "verdicts," to a butcher named Godin, one of the crowd of killers (632–33). Here, Schama sounds more like a prosecuting attorney than a historian. Obviously, the Nuremberg trials have changed our perspective on political crimes, so that even after more than two hundred years the perpetrators cannot escape detection and condemnation.

Writing about the uprising in Vendée, one of the bloodiest episodes of the Revolution, Schama gives yet another reason for his outrage: "The exterminations practiced there were . . . the logical outcome of an ideology that progressively dehumanized its adversaries and that had become incapable of seeing any middle ground between total triumph and utter eclipse" (792). In other words, you turn your adversaries into *Untermenschen* so that you can justify their slaughter. This judging of the past by the standards of the present is a remarkable feature of postmodern history. The past and the present mirror each other. Rejecting the role of an "objective," insensitive, morally uninvolved witness, Schama again follows the practice of Romantic historiography: the recovered past is a lesson for the present. By his angry condemnation the historian reinforces the general aversion people feel today when faced with horrendous crimes perpetrated in the name of a political mission.

## 3.2. EXCAVATING THE PAST: *LANDSCAPE AND MEMORY*

In chapter II, I focused on the structural differences between historical and fictional worlds. But when it comes to the entities that enter into world formation, the two types of worlds are homomorphous. In an earlier work (Doležel 1998) I divided the entities into two domains: the domain of nature, lacking intentionality, and the domain of intentionally acting agents, both individuals and groups. Historical worlds display the same two-domain structure: in the past, just as in the present, persons and social groups pursued intentional actions and interactions in the environment of nature states and intentionless nature events.[20] Although history is sometimes narrowly understood as a reconstruction of the past *human* acting, historiography has never neglected nature as the setting of human acting; not only geography but also climate and weather have been recognized as important factors in the shaping of human history.[21]

### *3.2.1. The Excavation Method*

Schama's *Landscape and Memory* is one of those rare books in which nature in its various forms is the dominant constituent of the historical world. Moreover, Schama reverses the traditional relationship between space and time: fixing the space, he treats time not as linear (horizontal) but as vertical. *Citizens* is a chronicle; its plot structure basically follows the chronology of the reconstructed events. In *Landscape and Memory* chronology is discarded. Instead of reconstructing the past as a sequence of events in linear time, Schama uncovers it by "digging" into space, into a location.[22] The historical world is constructed by stacking up selected, discontinuous time strata. The historian himself calls his method "excavation": "A curious excavator of traditions stumbles over something protruding above the surface of the commonplace of contemporary life. He scratches away, discovering bits and pieces of a cultural design that seems to elude coherent reconstruction but which leads him deeper into the past." The excavation, "beginning with the familiar," proceeds by "digging down through layers of memories and representations toward the primary bedrock, laid down centuries or even millennia ago, and then working up again toward the light of contemporary recognition" (16–17).[23]

The primary bedrock of history is constituted by "nature and landscape myths," whose beginnings are lost in time but whose momentous impact has persisted throughout human history. These myths are elementary, primary narratives of the interface between humans and nature, or more precisely, of the human transformation of nature into landscape. This transformation is not "simply the work of the industrial centuries. It has been happening since the days of ancient Mesopotamia" (7), indeed since the human species first appeared on the earth. By their perceptions, then by their representations, and finally by their interventions humans shape nature into landscape. The history of humankind, of the various races, nations, and cultures, occurs within specific landscapes.[24] Three elements in particular—wood, water, and rock—provide the environment for human history and, consequently, dominate Schama's excavated world.

Although the world of *Landscape and Memory* is primarily the world of inanimate elements, human agents are present in it. But the decisive reason for including certain individuals in the historical world is not their significance for general history but the fact that their life stories were in some essential way connected with the history of landscape creation. Sir Walter Ralegh, the searcher for El Dorado; John Taylor, the poet of the Thames; Bernini, the master fountain builder; Gutzon Borglum, the sculptor of the Mount Rushmore monument; Silanus Denecourt, who marked the forest trails at Fontainebleau; the "conquerors" of Mont Blanc. They are, so to speak, the frontline soldiers of the human effort to transform nature into landscape.

Schama's term *landscape* is undoubtedly honorific; it carries a hortatory connotation, expresses an aesthetic attitude and an existential optimism. It allows him to position his historiography both along and opposite contemporary environmental history. While acknowledging that "environmental history offers some of the most original and challenging history now being written," Schama objects to its "dismal tale" of "land taken, exploited, exhausted." He excavates a more complicated tale: "the richness, antiquity, and complexity of our landscape tradition. . . . Instead of assuming the mutually exclusive character of Western culture and nature, I want to suggest the strength of the links that have bound them together" (14).[25]

The basic pattern of Schama's excavation method is demonstrated in the first episode of the book, in the excavation of the past of the primeval forest Bialowieża (in the prologue and pt. 1, ch. 1). The story of the forest is set against the background of the tumultuous history of Poland and Lithuania. Schama's excavation starts in the present, with a personal visit to the region in search of the traces of his Jewish Lithuanian ancestors in 1992. At the very beginning of chapter 1 Schama discovers the emblem of the forest, the European bison *(żubr)*, and the animal becomes the core of his historical world. The excavator takes on the mantle of a literary historian and descends into the sixteenth century to bring to light a Latin ode to the bison written by a Polish visitor to Renaissance Rome, Nikolas Hussovski (Hussovianus). The story then turns "upwards," passing through several significant or emblematic episodes: a royal hunt, precisely dated (September 27, 1752); reforms in forestry management by King Stanislas, the last king of independent Poland (in the 1770s); the appointment in September 1820 of Julius von Brincken as the chief forester of Bialowieża; and the majestic celebration of the Lithuanian culture and landscape in Adam Mickiewicz's *Pan Tadeusz* (1834). As Poland suffers through nineteenth- and twentieth-century uprisings and wars, the forest becomes increasingly both a part and a symbol of this bloody history. It was a refuge for defeated rebels and soldiers, was hunted (and managed) by Hermann Göring, and in the late 1950s became the favorite hunting ground of Nikita Khrushchev. Schama turns again to literature to convey "the sense of directionless chagrin" of Polish history in the poetry of Tadeusz Konwicki (62) and in Stefan Żeromski's poetry, "swimming in mystical allusions to a sacred past and a sylvan destiny" (66).

Schama's story of Bialowieża and its bison ends where it started, in the writer's present. After a night spent in the forest Schama rises at dawn, "hoping to catch some of the wild bison herd on the move. . . . The bison failed to materialize." The historian takes a walk in the forest, on the surface of a landscape that hides "graves unmarked on the tourist maps, unknown bodies beneath the leafmold" (74). The present and the past are indissolubly linked in the historical strata piled under the feet of the historian of memory.

The plot structure of the history of Bialowieża reminds us of the *narratio modo Homerico,* the ancient narration *in medias res),* but it differs from it in that it starts not in the "middle" of the story but at the end.[26] A much loser plot is provided by the "meandering" path of excavation. This mode of construction is especially typical of part 2, "Water," as if the historian were inspired by the meandering flow of the Nile or a walk through the gardens of a Renaissance palace.[27] The historical world is a colorful mixture of discrete episodes and vignettes, reminding us of a postmodern collage.

The world of Water is formed by two main constituents: rivers and fountains. The meandering string of rivers follows the sequence Nile (ch. 5, sec. 1)—Jordan (sec. 3)—Nile (sec. 3)—Tiber (sec. 4)—Thames (sec. 4)—Tiber (sec. 5)—Danube, Nile, Ganges, Rio de la Plata (in Bernini's *Fountain of the Four Rivers*) (sec. 6)—Nile (sec. 6)—Orinoco (ch. 6, sec. 1)—Thames (sec. 2)—Bidassoa (sec. 3)—Thames (sec. 4)—Rhone (sec. 4)—Rhine (sec. 5)—Hudson (sec. 5)—Schuylkill (ch. 6, sec. 5)—Nile (sec. 6). There are obviously "favorite" rivers, especially the Nile and the Thames. There are also neglected rivers, particularly the rivers of Central Europe: the Danube is only mentioned, the Labe (Elbe) and the Visla did not make it onto Schama's map, and the mention of the Vltava (Moldau) contains an error.[28] The Nile-Thames axis is reemphasized in the conclusion: in the story of two voyages between England and Egypt, one of the adventurous transportation of the "Cleopatra" obelisk, the other of English tourists to Philae. The fountains follow the sequence Italy (ch. 5, sec. 4)—England and France (Caus) (sec. 4)—Rome (sec. 5)—Holland (sec. 5)—Rome (Bernini) (sec. 6)—Vaux-le-Vicomte—Versailles (ch. 6, sec.

3)—Caserta (sec. 3). The strains of rivers and fountains intersect in the "confluence" of Bernini's masterwork, the *Fountain of the Four Rivers.*

Schama's method of excavation frees the historian from the traditional yoke of chronology and opens for him many alternative patterns of "stringing" the events. In cases such as the reconstruction of the Bialowieża history it is the significance of the event for the given location that leads to its inclusion in the string. But in the meandering pattern the collage is formed by various kinds of associations, often quite tenuous. Thus, the Rhone is inserted into the sequence of rivers only by an accidental mention of the name Macaulay (355). The fountains of Renaissance Rome provide a thematic link to the Ghent-located art of the brothers van Eyck and Gerard Horenbout (287–88). The fountains of Versailles lead to the remarkable waterworks of Caserta just because Louis XIV's great-grandson was installed as king of Naples.

A more organized pattern of excavation returns in chapter 7, the first half of part 3, "Rock." Reconstructing the struggle for the conception and completion of the sculpted heads on Mount Rushmore, a monument to America's greatness, Schama comments: "To make over a mountain into the form of a human head is, perhaps, the ultimate colonization of nature by culture, the alteration of landscape to manscape" (396). Starting with this event of the 1930s, Schama descends to the Macedonian architect Dinocrates, who presented to Alexander the Great a monumental project: to carve Mount Athos into a gigantic statue of the king, complemented on his right by a city and on his left by a bowl receiving all the waters of the mountain (402). Many centuries later, in the time of the Renaissance pope Alexander VII, Dinocrates' vision was etched on paper by the Italian artist Pietro da Corona. In 1721 the German baroque architect Johann Bernard Fischer included in his book on historical architecture an engraving titled *The Mount Athos Colossus.* An impressive landscape showing the Mount Athos monument to Alexander was painted by Pierre-Henri de Valenciennes in 1796 (404). Dinocrates' project remained alive, but "no mountain colossi had actually been carved in the West" (405). In excavating the Dinocrates tradition, Schama has to transcend the domain of Western culture, pointing to the "many Buddhas carved into the hillsides of the southern [Chinese] province of Fukien by Sung dynasty monks sometime during the ninth century A.D." (406).

Expanding the theme of the carved mountain to the theme of sacred mountains, Schama glides easily from Chinese Taoist paintings to actual Christian "holy mounds" whose "archetypal parable" was repeated "in images and narratives of ascent" (415). Indeed the parable of ascent replaced the original Christian myth of the mountaintop as the site of battles between good and evil. The monks who built their monasteries in high mountains conquered evil. Visual artists of the Low Countries, Dante in his *Purgatorio,* and Petrarch in his description of the ascent of Mont Ventoux all encountered spiritual heights on a mountaintop. From Petrarch's narrative Schama shifts again to visual representations, emphasizing the stylized character of mountain landscapes sketched by Leonardo and painted by Peter Breugel the Elder. Bruegel's *The Dark Day* (1565) presents a pre-postmodern impossible world, a "whole succession of arbitrarily stitched together, discrete landscapes: Flemish cottages, Mediterranean river mouth, and Alpine needle-peaks" (431). The painting defies, indeed challenges, mimetism, just as Schama's excavation and meandering defy the chronological mimesis of traditional historiography.[29]

The constituents of the historical worlds centered around the element rock are a most diverse collection: carvings and statues, paintings and engravings, artificial "sacred mountains" and commercial mountain shows, fantastic tales, epic poems and Romantic fictions, narratives of pilgrimages, mountaineering books and philosophical arguments, and finally historical reconstructions of actual explorations, surveys, and conquests. In creating this multimedia collage Schama displays remarkably broad cultural knowledge and amazing versatility as a historian and writer. His historical world is a triumph of the freedom afforded to the postmodern excavator.

### *3.2.2. Schama's Mythography*

In the previous section I quoted Schama's statement that the primary bedrock of history reached by the excavation method is constituted by "nature and landscape myths." Not surprisingly, these myths and their transformations form the core of the historical world of *Landscape and Memory*. Schama, always aware of his own methodology and conception, reflects on the nature and study of myth, but just as is the case of his metahistory, these reflections are not espoused systematically but scattered throughout the book.

Schama's mythography is defined in opposition to the Enlightenment and positivist attitude, popularized most recently by James Frazer, according to whom myths "were simply 'mistakes' that primitives make about their world (and especially the natural world), mistakes committed in the grip of ignorance and fear." With the progress of "scientific, empirically derived knowledge" "the vitality and authority of nature religions declined" (209, 208), until, ultimately, myth and modern culture became mutually exclusive.

However, Schama observes, "myths are seductive things. A truly disconcerting number of those who have spent their lives codifying, narrating, and explicating them have not gone unbewitched by their spell" (133). Schama names Friedrich Nietzsche, Carl Jung, Joseph Campbell, and Mircea Eliade as representative of those thinkers who considered "myth and modernity not at all irreconcilable." For Jung, "to embrace myth and to readmit primitive religion in social behavior was not . . . to flee modernity but to face up to it" (209). Schama acknowledges the power of this argument but criticizes both its epistemological assumptions and its ideological consequences. He aligns himself with Carlo Ginzburg ("a fearsome prosecutor in these matters") and with his criticism of Georges Dumézil, who "failed to make a clear critical distance between himself and his subject [the German myths]" (134). The ideological consequences that Schama abhors are the myth devotees' totalitarian tendencies in their thinking about political and social issues of our time. Their "embrace of myth fired their hostility to natural-rights individualism, and the democratic politics that protects it" (134).

According to Schama, nobody struggled with the dilemma of myth and modernity more painfully than the art historian Aby Warburg. At the beginning of his scholarly career "Warburg concerned himself with showing the comparable processes by which primitive myth and magic had evolved a symbolic repertoire expressed in Renaissance art and sculpture" (210). Observing Hopi Indian rituals and ceremonies in New Mexico, Warburg "suddenly grasped the timeless universalism of the way symbols operate in our cultural consciousness" (211). Referring to his last work, a brief essay on tree cults, Schama takes this "assimilated German Jew" as his "guide" and argues, "against the grain of much environmental writing, that Western culture, even while it has been busy destroying forests, has been full, not drained, of such myths" (213).

Clearly speaking *pro domo sua,* Schama asks a question that is extremely topical in the postmodern age: "How much myth is good for us?" And he gives a most instructive answer: "Not to take myth seriously in the life of an ostensibly 'disenchanted' culture like our own is actually to impoverish our understanding of our shared world. And it is also to concede the subject by default to those who have no critical distance from it at all, who apprehend myth not as a historical phenomenon but as an unchallengeable perennial mystery" (134). Schama's approach affords the myth its proper historical significance but protects the explorer from succumbing to its seduction.

Schama's epistemology of myth study is in harmony with his general metahistory. It reasserts his conviction that the postmodern historian has to be intimately involved with his subject, while preserving his integrity in the reconstruction of the past. It is counterproductive to succumb to the ideology of the myth when pursuing a scholarly study of the myth. Early in his book Schama quotes "the great Talmudist" Saul Lieberman's comment on the study of Jewish mysticism: "Nonsense (when all is said and done) is still nonsense. But the study of nonsense, that is science" (134). This epistemological principle, despite its somewhat coarse language, applies generally to humanistic study; Schama strengthens our belief that it has not lost its validity in the postmodern age.

*3.2.3. Nature Myths and Their Transformations*

In accordance with Schama's epistemological position *Landscape and Memory* does not preach myths but shows their complex evolution, their historical transformations, transfigurations, and recodings, and reveals their hidden, symbolic presence in contemporary culture.[30]

The second section of part 1, with the Heideggerian title "Der Holzweg," is a remarkable intertwining of two related stories, the fate of the manuscript of Tacitus's *Germania* and the formation and transformations of the "Teutonic" myth in German culture. Tracing the development and growing popularity of this myth in German ideology, literature, and the visual arts, Schama points out its origins in the cult of the forest, the "typical" German landscape. While the Polish-Lithuanian forest was an ultimate refuge from history, the German forest is at the very heart, at the very core, of culture and history: "The German woods were more than simply an economic resource: they were in some mysteriously indeterminate way an essential element of the national character; they were, as Riehl put it, 'what made Germany German'" (116).[31] The Teutonic myth was first placed at the center of German culture by patriotic humanists (such as Conrad Celtis) who offered a revalorization of Tacitus's contrast between the Roman "civilization" and the Germanic "barbarism." Arminius (Hermann), the scourge of Varus's legions, becomes a hero of German patriotism and nationalism. The cult of the "Arminian" forest, first expressed in German literature and ideology, leads to the emergence of the German landscape painting, which, in the spirit of German nationalism, challenges the Italian manner. In his drawings, woodcuts, and paintings, especially in the "astonishing" *St. George and the Dragon* (ca. 1510), Albrecht Altdorfer "managed exactly to produce images of German trees and woods that in their startlingly dense and writhing forms proclaimed an unmistakable difference from anything attempted in Italian art" (99).

The inclusion of landscape painting expands substantially the scope of Schama's historical world. In contrast to the sketchy, superficially drawn domain of literary history, Schama's original analyses and interpretations of visual arts, which are models of the fusion of the aesthetic and the ideological, construct an essential domain of his historical world. The historical links in this domain lead from Altdorfer's *St. George* through the Romantic painter Caspar David Friedrich's *Chasseur in the Forest* (1813) to Anselm Kiefer's *Varus* (1976).[32] The German forest is a continual inspiration for German visual art, which keeps transforming aesthetically and ideologically the foundational myth of German nationalism.

Schama, who has never concealed his personal opinions about historical tragedies, reveals that "the long, undeniable connections between the mythic memory of the forest and militant nationalism have created a zone of great moral angst in Germany" (119). The national, tribal myth has a "fateful implication": it is "a force hard to resist, but which leads up the forest path, to a wooden grave" (133).

The English "greenwood" appears in the historical world of *Landscape and Memory* in chapter 3. It "entered the popular imagination in a quite different style from the primeval woods of Polish Lithuania or the German silva Hercynia" (140). Besides the legendary outlaw Robin Hood (in the later versions of the *Geste* legalized as the king's servant and protector), one can hardly find any myths or mythical beings in these "thin[ner] and almost patchy" woodlands (143). And when the theme of the forest morphs into the theme of timber (to which most of the pages of the chapter are devoted), we are mostly in a political, economic, or military history of forest exploitation instead of in the cultural history of the landscape and its myths.

In contrast to its English counterpart, the North American forest (and the North American landscape in general) early on became the subject of intensive mythologization. Soon after their discovery by the white man, the sequoias of Yosemite were transformed from a tourist attraction into a subject of veneration: "Yosemite became a symbol of a landscape that was beyond the reach of sectional conflict [the American Civil War], a primordial place of such transcendent beauty that it proclaimed the gift of the Creator to his new Chosen People" (191). In the minds of the American mythmakers, the monuments of European culture pale in comparison with the beauties of American nature (195). Painters of the first generation born in America "produced a number of landscapes in which great trees (usually oaks) figure as both heroic and spiritual actors in the scenery" (196). The painters were joined by writers and poets in proclaiming that "it is from this primordial vegetable matter, celestially sanctified and unspoiled yet by the touch of man, that America was born" (201).

American mythmaking is, in fact, a recent transplanting of the Christian nature myth. Schama "excavates" the origins of the Christian "vegetable theology" in the general grafting of "Christian theology onto preexisting pagan cults of nature" authorized by Pope Gregory the Great at the beginning of the seventh century (216). What followed was the most massive fusion in the history of myth. In this "hijacking of pagan myths" the symbolism of the ancient tree cults was grafted onto the cult of the Cross. "The miraculous transformation of dead into living wood supplied one of the most prolific motifs of the Christian tradition" (218, 220). "The verdant cross" became an enduring visual symbol of Christ's suffering, death, and resurrection.

The most comprehensive "excavation" in *Landscape and Memory* reconstructs the myth of Arcadia (in pt. 4, concentrated in ch. 9). The meandering method creates a fragmented world crowded with fascinating episodes and vignettes, among them an abandoned World War II air shelter, Hampstead Heath ("one of Romanticism's holy places"), the

Greek Pan myth and Virgil's Georgic scenes, Pliny's villas, Philip Sidney's (1633) and Jacopo Sannazaro's (1519) poems. It is a "flat" world, since all the fragments are treated as equally significant, whether they reconstruct momentous transformations or small, local changes.

This characterization of the historical world of part 4 applies, I believe, to all the worlds of *Landscape and Memory.* The book represents Schama's most radical postmodern writing, fusing without integrating traditional and new modes of historiography: dynastic and everyday life, political revolutions and cultural history (art and literary works, both masterpieces and ordinary fare), decisive battles and personal biographies, the history and mythology of nature.

*3.2.4. The Historiographer in His Historical World*

We observed already in *Citizens* (above, in sec. 3.1) a heightened subjectivization of the historian's discourse, both in the quantity and in the affective intensity of *Ich*-form digressions and commentaries or condemnations. In *Landscape and Memory* the reader is assured by *Ich*-form statements that on his complex, meandering and zigzag journeys into the past he or she is accompanied constantly by a reliable, witty, and humane guide. These *Ich*-form digressions are a traditional "license" of the historian.[33] The historian's irony and anger in *Citizens* are also centered on the level of the text. However, in *Landscape and Memory* the subjectivization proceeds from the text to the historical world by a clearly postmodern innovation. Schama imitates the method of metafiction.[34] In parallel with the story of the landscape runs, in reconstructed fragments, the author's life story: his childhood on the bank of the Thames and in London (3–4, 517), the exploration of an abandoned World War II air shelter (517–19), dining on whitebaits with his father (353), the journeys to Bialowieża (prologue) and to the California Redwoods (epilogue to pt. 1). It is tempting to call this mode of historical writing metahistory, but that is impossible given Hayden White's appropriation of the term for the theory or philosophy of history. We shall simply speak about the historian's own story and file it among the features of postmodern historiography. In this feature, the influence of the fictional on the historical narrative in the postmodern era is revealed very clearly.

## 3.3. FICTIONALIZING THE PAST: *DEAD CERTAINTIES (UNWARRANTED SPECULATIONS)*

*Dead Certainties (Unwarranted Speculations)* (1991) is a work of fiction, but it is fiction written by a principled professional historian. Schama announces the genre of the work not by a subtitle but by another paratextual device, his statements in the afterword and in the notes on sources. He characterizes the book as "a work of the imagination that chronicles historical events" (327). It should not be judged as a piece of scholarship, of historiography: "Although both [stories] follow the documented record with some closeness, they are works of the imagination, not scholarship. Both resolve the certainties of events into the multiple possibilities of alternative narrations" (320). Two kinds of passages are "purely imagined fiction": "In the first kind (as in the soldier's witness of the Battle of Quebec) the narrative has been constructed from a number of contemporary documents. The more purely fictitious dialogues (such as Marshal Tukey's conversation with Ephraim Littlefield) are worked up from my own understanding of the sources as to how such a scene might have taken place" (327). The phrase "how such a scene might have taken place" is crucial to understanding Schama's method of world construction in this work: his is a fictional world, but the constructing imagination is inspired by "documents" or by the historian's "understanding of sources."[35]

The author's statements define not only the main purpose of the book—to provide multiple alternative representations of a historical event—but also its strategy—to derive fictional worlds from historical ones. The historian is fully committed to his sources but enhances and complements them by a deliberate, acknowledged fictionalization. To an orthodox postmodern theorist the method confirms that the boundary between historical and fictional representations is erased. But to a critical analyst it represents just a new phase in an ancient tradition: fusing history and fiction in the genre of historical fiction (see chapter IV).[36]

### *3.3.1. Two Deaths of the General*

At least since Leopold Ranke, historians have struggled with a depressing problem: "the wide divergences between the various accounts" of one and the same event (Barnes 1962, 245). Even primary sources show these divergences, which are exacerbated by the different, often contradictory representations of the past in historiographic writings. The first story in *Dead Certainties,* entitled "The Many Deaths of General Wolfe," is a narrative of this trauma of the historian, a collage of primary and secondary historical representations recounting different versions of one and the same historical event. The first and last of the five sections are primary sources—accounts of witnesses; the second and fourth sections are secondary representations, one by an anonymous historian, the other by the American historian Francis Parkman. The third section offers to view a fictional representation, a historical painting executed by Benjamin West. The sections are discontinuous in their linear sequence, but we can see a "deep" structuring in a symmetrical pattern: A–B–C–B–A. In narrating directly or indirectly the events that led to the death of General Wolfe on the battlefield of the Heights of Abraham and the death itself, Schama's collage constructs a fictional representation of the precarious foundations of historiography.

The first section, "At the Face of the Cliff," is a first-person narrative of an English soldier, a member of the detachment dispatched to climb up the cliff and attack the French encampment on the Heights. The event is exactly localized and dated: "Anse du Foulon, Quebec, four a.m., September 13, 1759." The narrative reads like a diary entry but is composed at a later, unspecified time. It gives us our first glimpse of General Wolfe as seen by his soldiers: "He was a good general to trust, even if it was his fancy to call us 'brother soldiers,' for he was fearless and would walk before the men under fire" (7). The soldier's story is also the first manifestation of Schama's method of multiple representations. The soldier contradicts the posthumous myth of the General: "After he died they made him look like a Roman, even on the penny prints I have seen, but he looked no Roman to us. For though he was six foot, he carried that height queerly, in a loping gait, with his bony frame and sloping shoulders ending in a poke-up neck. What was on top of it bore little resemblance to the Antiques either, what with his pop eyes and his little chins wobbling under his jaw, his skin the colour of cheese and a snout on him like a ferret. Nor was he much a humorous man, more in the melancholy way" (7).

The second section, "The Life of General Wolfe," an authoritative third-person biography interspersed with passages from the General's correspondence and occasional reports of his thoughts, authenticates the soldier's portrayal. It provides a brief account of Wolfe's family background, his upbringing and military career, but its main focus is the reconstruction of his personal traits. He is presented as a typical pre-Romantic character, fragile in body and sentimental in spirit: "Wolfe was always more than a waver of flags and a rattler of sabers. His driven, febrile personality, swinging between tender compassion and angry vanity, was haunted by Night Thoughts, by ravens perched on tombstones. If he was an empire-builder he knew he was also a grave-digger, perhaps his own" (18). Indeed, the trials and tribulations of the Quebec campaign brought the General to the brink of the grave: "But now, he thought, he was dying, withering away of gravel and consumption; a raging, scalding venom that ate at his guts" (12). In this state, death on the battlefield was the best way out for a victorious commander.

"In Command," the third section, is an art-historical analysis of Benjamin West's painting *The Death of General Wolfe,* which finalized the General's "Roman" image. The master of historical painting unveiled this remarkable work at the Royal Academy Exhibition Gallery in Pall Mall on April 29, 1771. Although it was a great success, it stirred up a controversy, because West had not followed the conventions of classicist art but had pursued historical "truth," at least as he saw it (27). At the same time, however, he expressed the aesthetics of his work quite clearly: "All should be proportioned to the highest idea conceived of the Hero. . . . A mere matter of fact will never produce the effect" (28). The art historian's deconstruction of the painting confirms that West achieved his goal: "Throughout the composition, from top to bottom, mere fact is overwhelmed by inspired, symbolically loaded invention. It was this unapologetic hyperbole which set West's painting off so dramatically from the prosaic versions that precede it" (28). Comparing the cast of characters surrounding the dying Wolfe with historical evidence, Schama does not miss the opportunity to indulge in postmodern irony: "The most startling fiction of all was the Indian, posed in the Antique form of poetic contemplation, precisely the quality commonly denied to the 'Savages,' as they were invariably called by the British of Wolfe's generation. The General himself had considered them to be irredeemable barbarians, cruel and deprived. What is more they fought, exclusively, for the other side. . . . The bizarre notion that Wolfe would have tolerated their presence at the moment of his apotheosis would have been a bitter jest to anyone familiar with his prejudices" (30–31).

West's historical canvas reconfirms graphically the opposition between historical and fictional representations. While the mythologization of history might seem an innocent fictional enterprise, it has a fatal impact. In popular beliefs myth replaces history: "The success of the painting . . . had been such that when British children of future generations grew up drilled in the pieties of imperial history, it was West's scene they imagined rather than any more literal account. Art had entirely blotted out mere recall, let alone evidence" (37). We glimpse the debate about fiction and history from a new angle: the erasure of their opposition is tantamount to, or perhaps inspired by, popular cognitive appropriations of historical fiction. Historical fiction is mistaken for a "true" representation of the past.

The fourth section, "Deep in the Forest," approaches the story of General Wolfe in a roundabout way. The primary focus of this section is the life and scholarly development of the prominent nineteenth-century American historian Francis Parkman (see above, sec. 3.2.1). Its main part is a synopsis of Parkman's autobiography, which recounts not only his intellectual growth and professional accomplishments but also his physical and mental feebleness; it is a "self-portrait of a creature in pain" (44). One link to Wolfe's story is that Parkman's pioneering work *France and England in North America* provides a broader context for Wolfe's campaign and death. A more intimate link is the empathic fusion of the historian and his subject accomplished by the Romantic historian's passionate immersion in the past: "Past and present dissolved at this moment. He became Wolfe and Wolfe lived again through him" (64). Parkman's story becomes a strain of Wolfe's story.

What kind of account provides the fusion of the historian's and the subject's stories? Let me first point out that by the consensus of his contemporaries Parkman was a master of "painting in paragraphs, of recreating the identities of La Salle and Champlain, Montcalm and Wolfe, of tracking their destinies through the forests and river valleys of pristine North America, of giving meaning to their lives and deaths" (43). Parkman and Wolfe's America is an unspoiled landscape of cedar, red oak, and pine forests. The forest is "the principal character" of Parkman's history of America (48; see also above, sec. 3.2.3). In this setting, the confrontation between England and America in the war of 1756–63 is "as epic as anything recorded in the annals of Greece and Rome. The climax of their encounter, on the Heights of Abraham, was, he [Parkman] imagined, one of those moments in which a whole universe now remote in its values and virtues was reformed into the shape required by modern empires. Wolfe and Montcalm were, then, chivalric figures; incarnations of duty, sacrifice and resolution; doomed, both victor and vanquished, to perish before a world which had brushed those fancies aside" (49). The parallel between the historian, Parkman, and his hero, Wolfe, reveals that their lives and deaths share the same pattern, carry the same meaning: "to compel his feeble body to bear him till the work is done" (64).

The symmetrical pattern of Schama's textual collage is completed by the first-person narrative "On the Heights of Abraham," dated "Nine a.m., September 13, 1759." The narrator is a British soldier who is sent by his commander to report to the General that the British have held their line and put the enemy to flight. Now we read the Ur-source of all the accounts of Wolfe's death: "I suddenly saw him, lying on a mound beside a sorry little bush attended by just two men, one leaning over and supporting Wolfe with his arm. . . . I approached Wolfe and saw his face had gone stiff and greenish and his red hair glistened with sun and sweat. Blood had matted his belly where another ball had struck him and now more was oozing through his shirt and coat, so seeing he would not live I told him our news and in a groaning, gurgling sort of way I could hear him praise God for it" (69).[37]

The story is finished, but Schama's narrative continues. In an appendix-epilogue, the fictionalist-cum-historian quotes a letter dated October 25, 1759, written by Katherine Lowther, whom Wolfe planned to marry, to Wolfe's mother, Mrs. Henrietta Wolfe. It is a posthistorical closure of Wolfe's life, of his irreconcilable dilemma between a romantic attachment and a stern mother's disapproval. Now Katherine has only "reverence and affection" for "the Hero's Mother" (70).

Although the title of the first narrative of *Dead Certainties (Unwarranted Speculations)* refers to "many deaths" of General Wolfe, a close reading reveals that there are only two representations of his death and, in general, of all the events of the past: *fact-rendering* and *myth-creating*. I suggest these terms to designate the distinction between accounts that strive for an accurate and unbiased representation of a past event and those that transform the past event into an episode of some grand sacred, national, cultural, or philosophical narrative. The former write history; the latter, myths, explanations or justifications of collective beliefs. The individual sections of Schama's collage clearly split into these two kinds. In fact, there is an implicit polemic between the two conceptions. The soldier-narrator of the first section mentions "penny-prints" that created the "Roman" image of Wolfe. West's painting is a glamorous work of high art that finalized this mythical image. In "The Life of General Wolfe," Indians, fighting on the side of the French, brought "shuddering terror" to the British; in West's painting a philosophizing "noble Savage" bends before the dying British commander. The soldier-narrator of the fifth section states that in his last hours Wolfe was attended "by just two men" (69), whereas in West's painting the drama of the moment is witnessed by "three groups of officers arrayed like a Greek chorus" (30), not to mention the aforementioned Indian.[38] The polemic becomes a self-contradiction in Francis Parkman's history. It is based on piles of primary materials, yet its account is ultimately mythologizing: the war between the French and the British is seen as a Greek or Roman epic, Wolfe as a chivalric hero. Schama's collage of five texts constructs two incompatible fictional worlds, "two deaths" of General Wolfe.

### *3.3.2. History as Criminal Trial*

The first story in *Dead Certainties* is linked to the second story only by a fleeting cross reference in Francis Parkman's biography: "Uncle George Parkman, whose real estate speculations were notoriously profitable and who had written extensively on the care of lunatics, had just recently been murdered by a debtor of his who also happened to be a Harvard Professor of Chemistry" (57).

Schama's second story is about the shaky status of such "dead certainties" as the guilt of Professor Webster. It represents fictionally the historian's predicament by focusing on the analogy between historiography and judicial proceedings. The similarities between a historian's reconstruction of the past and a criminal court trial are obvious. Both require a careful examination of the evidence and, based on this evidence, the determination of what "actually" happened in the past. Criminal courts are the first historians of crime. They operate on the same principle as historiography: by choosing between competing narratives, between rival stories, and deciding which one is credible (249–50). They are also faced with the same dilemma: while some evidence seems to offer certainty of truth, further considerations might turn it again into uncertainty. Referring to the Webster trial and its aftermath, Schama writes: "Each time that some sort of finality was proclaimed, new uncertainties reappeared" (288).[39]

In "Death of a Harvard Man" Schama writes a narrative text that most remarkably serves the purpose of constructing an uncertain, shaky fictional world. It is a modern fictional narrative in McHale's sense (see the introduction). Its most typical devices are the subjectivized narrative mode, *Ich*-form narrative, represented discourse, interior monologue, and sudden shifts from one text type to another.

Traditional historical narrative asserts its "objectivity" and authority in the construction of historical worlds by applying the ancient "omniscient" mode of narration, the authoritative *Er*-form. The fictionalized history of the death of a Harvard man, like the story of the deaths of General Worlfe, does not avoid this narrative mode but abolishes its monopoly by narrating substantial portions of the story in other narrative modes. The "objectivity" of the *Er*-form narrative is often undermined by pronounced subjectivization relative to different participants (especially the protagonists) of the story. Thus arises a multiperspectival narrative, an account that does not privilege one, authenticated version of events but plays different versions against one another.

The subjectivization strikes the reader right from the beginning, from the first section, in which George Briggs, the governor of Massachusetts, agonizes over whether he should commute the death sentence and save John Webster's life or let him hang. The narrative is sprinkled with expressions of subjective attitudes whose source can only be the governor himself: "Much as he respected the stern proceedings of the trial, he was too much a lawyer himself (or perhaps too much of a smithy's son) to imagine that it told the whole story. The defense, after all, had opened with one account and closed with another—a fatal strategy" (81). Subjectivized *Er*-form shifts easily into the governor's interior monologue, expressed in represented discourse, as in the following self-defense against his detractors: "Him, a heathen, who had laboured the best part of his life to bring together the service of the state and the ministry of Christ! Him, hard-hearted, who had begun his career in the law defending a poor savage Indian against the rope" (74). We find subjective attitudes of other protagonists in other sections, for example, Marshal Tukey's in section 2: "The politicians were on his back again and every time Wendell Phillips opened his singsong mouth on the Common about Free-Soil and the slaves, people's heads got broken. Mayor Quincy was his friend alright but there would be a new mayor, a Bigelow, next year and he was not to be counted on" (119). A direct-discourse interior monologue can be recorded as a silent reaction to somebody else's speech, as in the defense attorney Bemis's unspoken comment on a speech by one of the prosecutors: "'Assume,' such a little word, Bemis thought. For gentlemen such as him and me and all the Harvard classmates sitting in this room, it signifies something hypothetical, suppositious, intellectually experimental. But, my learned friend and fool, you have assumed too much; you have used it for those good tradesmen and mechanics over there" (246).

Just as the subjectivized *Er*-form shifts imperceptibly into the represented discourse of interior monologue, so David Littelfield's interior monologue, expressed in direct discourse, shifts into *Ich*-form narrative: "They made their mark, all those niggling questions from the Marshal. You would think, wouldn't you, after all I'd done, that the Marshal might be more accommodating? . . . As for Webster, there had always been bad feeling between us, ever since I started as janitor seven years ago" (121). The *Ich*-form dominates Littlefield's account of his dig through the wall into Dr. Webster's laboratory and the subsequent discovery of the remains of a body. The *Ich*-form, a purely subjective narrative mode, recurring again and again, presses the main point of Schama's reconstruction of Dr. Webster's story: all the evidence presented at his trial, including the experts' reports, is subjective and therefore cannot establish "dead certain" facts of the case. Schama, a historian, has mastered the devices of modern fictional narrative, in which contradictory subjective accounts are means of concealment, of preserving a "mystery" at the core of the story, a mystery that perhaps can never be solved.

Only at the conclusion of the story, Webster's surprising confession, made just before his execution, seems to provide "the truth of the case, the ultimate nugget of certainty that historians once imagined they could find if only they looked hard and long enough in the archives" (293). But this attainment of certainty is immediately followed by new uncertainties. Although the confession, conveyed by lengthy quotations of Webster's own words, has, "in essence, the ring of truth," it is reported solely by the minister who elicited it. And the subsequent experts' reports are contradictory: "Can a man be killed instantaneously with a blow from a piece of wood? Impossible, said one set of doctors who came to testify to the Council; quite possible, if not likely, said another set, citing the fragility of the temples and Dr. Parkman's particularly brittle cranial structure" (293).

The unstable *Er*-form narrative, again and again subjectivized by incursions of various personal attitudes, long passages of personal *Ich*-form, frequent direct discourse or represented discourse, and interior monologues of many participants are complemented by several other text types: a synopsis of Webster's written document (presented to his lawyers) with some exact quotations; dialogues between attorneys and witnesses in different forms of speech (direct, indirect, represented); Webster's own testimony in direct discourse and in a third-person summation; résumés of the attorneys' presentations, interspersed with direct quotations; synopses of the witnesses' testimonies with some *Ich*-form quotations; the chief justice's charge to the jury in the typical pattern "direct discourse—third-person summation"; entries from an attorney's diary; letters; a journalist's report.[40] Verbal texts are complemented by drawings and photographs of evidence. The account of the trial concludes with a text of yet another type, a comment written by an anonymous juror the next week: "What a relief it was to us when we were again allowed to 'go free' and rejoin our families and friends after so long and painful a separation! And there was not a Juror's heart but would have leapt for joy could the prisoner have been justly allowed the same unspeakable blessing" (273). In this diversity of text types, in this textual collage, Schama's modern narrative devices turn into vehicles of postmodern fiction (see IV.4).

This collage is enriched by yet another narrative mode, the rhetorical *Er*-form expressing evaluative comments originating with the narrator: "It was a well-done opening, no doubt" (207); "Marshal Tukey was first at the stand, looking crisp as fresh laundry" (209). Rendering the closing stage of the trial, the rhetorical narrator, in the best tradition of his craft, pronounces a maxim, an assessment that sums up the uncertainty of Dr. Webster's crime but transcends the narrated situation and relates to the world outside the story: "It is impossible to know how men will conduct themselves under the domination of passion in its highest excitement" (247).[41] But the most surprising intervention is a clearly anachronistic rhetorical question provoked by an account of the conditions in nineteenth-century French insane asylums: "Was this not admirable, Michel Foucault?" (99).

It cannot escape our attention that in the concluding paragraphs, as the story leaps from the past to the present, another device of postmodern narrative appears: a metafictional switch from an anonymous narrator to a personalized narrator-author: "Two houses remain in my mind: the beginning and the end of a history. One of these houses I imagine set high on a cone-shaped hill overlooking a bay in the Azores. . . . The other house sits in blessed neglect, well off the beaten path of Harvard University tours" (315). The author has discarded the historian's role of a distanced observer of the past to assume the role of an involved author for whom the past is a melancholy recollection.

In a polemic with a majority of those in his profession Simon Schama writes: "Historians . . . have a vested interest in insisting that the past is a foreign country, since they like to claim a monopoly on translating its alien tongues. But sometimes they aren't needed. Sometimes the culturally conditioned response cracks apart and an emotion immediately recognizable to modern sensibilities makes itself felt" (1999, 145). Schama's empathy recognizes these cracks. Through them, he gets personally, almost physically close to the past, lives a surrogate life there surrounded by its people, messages, images. This is the main feature of Schama's recovery of the past; it allows him to be both "objective" and subjective, to engage both historical research techniques and fictional imagination, to construct both historical and fictional worlds without confusing them. For these reasons, his postmodern reconstructions of the past have already become classics.

CHAPTER 4

# Postmodern Historical Fiction

## 1. The World of Historical Fiction

The immensely popular literary genre of fictional representations of the past includes historical novels and romances, short stories, dramas, epic poems, and ballads, among other forms. The possible worlds of this genre are fictional, and they share the logical, semantic, structural, and pragmatic features of all fictional worlds. They also share with some other fictional worlds the dyadic structure, being composed of two domains that are clearly distinguishable by their different relationships to the actual world of the past (see Doležel 1998, 128–29). The first domain is made of fictional entities—acting persons, events, economic, political, and cultural conditions, physical settings, and so on—that do not have counterparts in the actual past. The second domain, which is, in fact, the defining feature of the genre, is constituted by fictional entities that have counterparts in actual historical agents, historical events, past economic, political, and cultural conditions, physical settings, and so on.[1] All entities in the world of historical fiction are fictional, but for the sake of distinctness, I use the term *fictional entities* for the first kind of world constituents and *fictionalized entities* for the second kind. The duality of the world entities is especially apparent in the case of the agential constellation: it is split into two subsets, one of fictional agents bearing the names of persons who existed and acted in the actual past—for example, Tolstoy's Napoleon—and one of fictionalized agents lacking such a property—for example, Tolstoy's Bezuchov, Stendhal's Sorel, Dickens's Darnay. The proper names of historical persons are special language expressions, rigid designators. As such, they insert into the fictional world a transworld-identical fictional counterpart of an actual character. This is precisely the origin of all fictionalized Napoleons—Tolstoy's, Stendhal's, Kayser's, and others'. As we know (see II.1), transworld morphing is a general transformation that affects all actual entities entering into fictional worlds: they have to change into fictional possibles. As a consequence, all fictional worlds, including worlds of historical fiction, are semantically homogeneous. According to the principle of semantic homogeneity, the Napoleons and the Kutuzovs of historical fiction can coexist, interact, and communicate with the Bezuchovs and the Sorels. If the agents were not semantically homogeneous, they would never be able to meet (see Doležel 1998, 16–18).

Semantic homogeneity warrants a unified dyadic world. However, the conceptual tools of possible-worlds semantics—cross-world identity lines, counterpart relationships, and proper names as rigid designators—encourage us to compare the fictional worlds of historical narratives with the historical worlds of the actual past to which they are attached or from which they are derived. Does this semantic correlation require the student of historical fiction to turn into a historian? I do not think so.

The prime task of historiography is to gather knowledge about the actual past by proposing historical worlds as models of the past. The prime task of historical fiction is to create fictional worlds that are alternatives to the model representations of the actual past; recall of historical knowledge is just a means of fictional-world construction. The fiction maker gathers as much historical knowledge as he or she wishes and transforms it in ways that correspond to the general order of the world under construction. The common reader does not have to recover all this knowledge. We can roughly distinguish three degrees of historical-knowledge recovery in the reception (reading and study) of historical fiction. In the first degree only the familiar knowledge of the past, the appropriate historical section of the common cultural encyclopedia, is invoked. It enables the reader to distinguish fictional entities from fictionalized entities and to determine how the entities of the second kind measure up to their actual-world counterparts in their generally known character traits and life stories. By this procedure he or she not only recognizes the dyadic design of the fictional world but can also decide whether the world is historically accurate, mythologizing, legendary, or counterfactual. Possible-worlds semantics justifies such a "naïve" reading: the world of a historical fiction is as sovereign and self-validated as the world of a psychological novel. A semantic analysis such as the one conducted in this chapter is based on this kind of reading. The second degree of the historical-knowledge recovery in a piece of historical fiction starts when the reader, spurred by the cross-world identical entities, wants to know more about the fictionalized past than the common cultural encyclopedia provides. After reading a piece of historical fiction (or seeing a historical movie), he or she "researches" available historical reconstructions, expanding his knowledge of the historical world on which the fiction is based. The study of sources used by the fiction maker in world construction is a special case of this degree of historical-knowledge recovery. This study, exemplified by Viktor Shklovsky's 1928 work on Tolstoy's *War and Peace,* is necessary for literary history, illuminating the genesis and, consequently, the meaning of the fictional world.[2] There is a third degree of the appropriation of historical knowledge: the fictional world is confronted with contemporary historical worlds that reconstruct the same period, events, and so on. We pursue this procedure if we ask how Dickens's *Tale of Two Cities* corresponds to our contemporary knowledge of the French Revolution or how Flaubert's *Salammbô* captures the history of Carthage as we know it today. I believe that the asking of such questions, whether by a student of literature or by a historian, is a manifestation of a mimetic attitude that treats historical fictions as historical documents. It is, in fact, an assessment of the reliability of historical fiction as a source of historical knowledge. This assessment violates the rights and freedoms of the fictional imagination in the construction of the past and would prevent the creation of anti-mimetic historical-fiction worlds; it is therefore incompatible with our conception of historical fiction. If a historian is tempted to use historical fiction as one of his or her documents, then he or she has to take into account the fact that no world in which fictional entities appear can be an adequate model of the past. We can be sure that no fictional agents acted in the past or influenced the shaping of historical events.[3]

## 2. Postmodern Historical Fiction

Authors of historical fiction presumably know the pertinent historical facts, but unlike their partners, historians, they are not bound by them. Only mimetic critics feel compelled to compare historical fictions with "what actually happened" and praise the fiction writers for being "truthful" to the past or shame them for "distorting" the past. Mimetic theory fails to account even for the so-called realistic historical fictions. It fails quite miserably when called on to account for the modern and the postmodern innovations. Only a semantics of fiction based on the idea of possible worlds can accept and interpret the radical experiments conducted by the postmodern makers of historical fiction.

In the realm of fiction, historical fact is a construct. That is why it has always been easy for writers of historical fiction to blend fictional and fictionalized persons, events, and so on, to create fictional documents of the past, to set an invented personal story in a fictionalized social context of the past. This flexibility blossoms into absolute liberty in the postmodern period. Historical fiction—from Thomas Pynchon's *Gravity's Rainbow* (1973) through Carlos Fuentes's *Terra Nostra* (1975), to Günter Grass's *Flounder* (1977)—becomes the most representative genre of postmodern literature.[4] Clearly, its authors cultivate a radically nonessentialist semantics (see II.2), which allows them to change even the most fundamental, individuating properties of historical persons, events, settings. According to Brian McHale, "traditional historical novels" strive "to hide the ontological 'seams' between fictional projections and real-world facts. They do so by tactfully avoiding contradictions between their versions of historical figures and the familiar facts of these figures' careers, and by making the background norms governing their projected worlds conform to accepted real-world norms" (1987, 17).[5] By contrast, a postmodern historical novel, such as Fuentes's *Terra Nostra*, "foregrounds its ontological seams by systematically transgressing these rules of its genre. Here familiar facts are tactlessly contradicted—Columbus discovers America a full century too late, Philip II of Spain marries Elizabeth of England, and so on—and the projected world is governed by fantastic norms" (17).[6] Postmodern historical fictions stage "transhistorical parties," "wholly unhistorical confrontations between two or more real-world figures": Kafka and Wittgenstein, young Jack Kennedy and Malcolm X, Richard Nixon and Ethel Rosenberg (85).[7] Readers and interpreters of this kind of fiction need a historical encyclopedia not to check the accuracy of the fictional facts but to discover their "deviant" postmodern alternatives.

Postmodern historical-fiction writers, unlike writers of traditional historical fiction, do not create fictional worlds that agree with the historical record; rather, they create alternative possible pasts. In this respect, and in this respect only, postmodern historical fiction is like falsified history (see II.3), the major distinction between them being that falsified history serves perverse political purposes, while postmodern historical fiction is an aesthetic game of unleashed imagination. The ultimate result is the creation of a richer, more varied, often more exciting past. The reader is forcefully reminded that the past of the world as he or she knows it is only one of many possible pasts. And the postmodern writer has the daring imagination to write them into existence.

Since historical fiction constructs historical facts *en masse,* could it not be recruited in support of the postmodern challenge? McHale thinks so: "The postmodernists fictionalize history, but by doing so they imply that history itself may be a form of fiction" (1987, 96). Malcolm Bradbury expressed this idea most elegantly: "As history is the lies the present tells in order to make sense of the past, I have improved it where necessary. I have altered the places where facts, data, info, seem dull or inaccurate. I have quietly corrected errors in the calendar, adjusted flaws in world geography, now and then budged the border of a country, or changed the constitution of a nation. I have elegantly replanned some of the world's greatest cities, moving buildings to better sites, redesigning architecture, opening fresh views and fine urban prospects, redirecting the traffic. I've put statues in more splendid locations, transferred or rehung famous paintings, staged entire new plays and operas. I have revised or edited some of our great books, and republished them" (2000, xxi). "Especially striking," according to McHale, "are the attitudes of paranoiac conspiracy-theorists like Pynchon and Reed, historians of the world's secret history, who seem intent on persuading us that their apparently crackpot accounts are closer to historical truth than those of supposedly responsible professional historians" (1987, 96).[8]

The most elaborate argument in favor of deriving a postmodern view of history from its historical fiction was developed by Linda Hutcheon (1988). Hutcheon sides with those who believe that postmodern historical fiction is fundamentally different from its "classic" predecessor. To emphasize this distinction, she designates the postmodern mutant "historiographic metafiction." While she tackles the notion in several sections of her study, in my view she characterizes it most clearly in the following:

> There is no abysmal infinite regress to absence or utter groundlessness in the fiction of Salman Rushdie or Ian Watson, or in the films of Peter Greenaway. The past really did exist. The question is: how can we know that past today—and what can we know of it? The overt metafictionality of novels like *Shame* or *Star Turn* acknowledges their own constructing, ordering, and selecting processes, but these are always shown to be historically determined acts. It puts into question, at the same time as it exploits the grounding of historical knowledge in the past real. This is why I have been calling this historiographic metafiction. It can often enact the problematic nature of the relation of writing history to narrativization and, thus, to fictionalization, thereby raising the same questions about the cognitive status of historical knowledge with which current philosophers of history are also grappling. What is the ontological nature of historical documents? Are they the stand-in for the past? What is meant—in ideological terms—by our "natural" understanding of historical explanation? Historiographic metafiction refutes the natural or common-sense methods of distinguishing between historical fact and fiction. It refuses the view that only history has a truth claim, both by questioning the ground of that claim in historiography and by asserting that both history and fiction are discourses, human constructs, signifying systems, and both derive their major claim to truth from that identity. (92–93)

Three tenets are fundamental to Hutcheon's argument: (1) The past actually existed. (2) The basic questions of contemporary philosophy of history are epistemic; they concern the reliability or even the possibility of cognitive representations of the past. (3) Historiographic metafiction raises the same epistemic questions that contemporary philosophy of history raises. It asserts that both history and fiction are discourses and that by writing the past both necessarily construct it. The narrativization of history further undermines its truth claim, because it is tantamount to fictionalization. Historiographic metafiction thus formulates a particular metahistory, and this metahistory happens to agree with the fundamental claims of the postmodern challenge.[9]

Unlike some postmodern radicals, Hutcheon does not deny actual existence to the past; she does not reduce it to the status of text. This allows her to distinguish between the past and its representations. Possible-worlds semantics has no qualms with her claim that both historical and fictional representations of the past are semiotic constructs ("signifying systems"). But we part company with her when she repeats the tautology that narrativization equals fictionalization (see ch. 1, sec. 1). If historiographic metafiction supports this tautology, then one has the right to ask how a piece of fiction can express a rather abstract argument concerning the epistemology of historiography. Wherefrom comes the authority of the fiction maker to decide what the principles of writing history are? How can we justify anthropomorphizing phrases when we state, for example, that fiction "refutes," "puts into question," or "acknowledges" a certain philosophical view? What I see here is an ideological position that tries to find its confirmation in fiction.

To be sure, fictional or nonfictional texts of fiction writers often comment on the "professional" issues of history or fiction writing or on literature in general. These statements are commonly interpreted as opinions of the author or at least as being close to the author's opinions. There is also no question that postmodern fiction makers are particularly fond of making such pronouncements, especially on the issue of fiction and history, and some of them ally themselves with the postmodern challenge. For example: "I present to you History, the fabrication, the diversion, the reality-obscuring drama. History, and its nearest relative, Histrionics" (Swift 1984, 34); "I said earlier that we are all poets, though not many of us write poetry; and so are we all novelists, that is, we have a habit of writing fictional futures for ourselves, although perhaps today we incline more to put ourselves into a film" (Fowles 1977, 295); "There is really no fiction or nonfiction; there is only narrative" (Doctorow 1999, xiv; see also the above quotation from Bradbury). But these fiction writers do not offer any argument or supporting evidence for their opinions. It makes sense to ask why the masters of fabulation who created such complex plots as that of *Ragtime* would express a simple, unoriginal theoretical opinion? Reading their historical novels, we become easily convinced that they are much more than parables of a certain philosophy of history.

One last point on the metahistorical import of postmodern historical fiction: Postmodernism, as we know from the introduction, is extremely accommodating with regard to earlier styles, ideas, and structures and thus achieves an extraordinary internal variety. "We look at a postmodernist building and see all the history of architecture as a possible quotation among its curves and arches. . . . We ask about the postmodern view of history, and we find all the responses of the history of historiography floating as potential responses. From this repository of possibilities one can draw what might be called a postmodern pattern book" (Thiher 1990, 10). A rich pattern book is, I believe, a more appropriate metaphor of postmodern fiction's metahistory than the image of an ideologically committed warrior.[10] If we have to derive a metahistory from postmodern historiographic metafiction, let us do it in the free postmodern spirit. Then we might discover many possible metahistories.

That I criticize the operation that reduces the astonishing diversity of postmodern fictional narratives to a dogmatic tenet of a philosophy of history does not mean that I dismiss the work of McHale and Hutcheon. On the contrary, theirs are the best books available on postmodern fiction, both firmly stating that postmodernism is a period of an extraordinary flourishing of fictional prose in general and historical fiction in particular. But in order to go beyond the abstract argument to the structural and aesthetic diversity of postmodern fiction, we have to follow these literary theorists not so much in their speculative theorizing as in their analyses of individual postmodern works. In other words, just as in chapter III, I propose here to look at a couple of representative works of postmodern historical fiction to see what a close reading can tell us about this fascinating transformation of the traditional genre. And as in chapter III, we shall examine not works of radical rewriting of history but works that might be called the moderate postmodern.

## 3. The Maturing of a Nation: E. L. Doctorow's *Ragtime*

There is a structural similarity between the fictional world of Doctorow's *Ragtime* (1974) and the historical world of Schama's *Citizens.* In both worlds we find two distinct domains of relatively equal importance: the domain of individual agents, performing individual actions and interactions, both private and public, and pursuing their particular life histories; and the domain of groups, organized or unorganized, involved in social actions and interactions and pursuing their collective goals, interests, and beliefs. We have seen that in Schama's world the groups become more and more active and play an ever-increasing role in the unfolding of the historical-world story (the story of the French Revolution) (see III.3). Doctorow's fictional world is reconfigured in a sudden shift from the predominance of individual acting to the predominance of social acting. The first part of the novel focuses on the private stories of the members of three families—Father's, Tateh's, and Sarah's. This world is not without conflict, tension, and suffering, but it is primarily a world of love and caring. It ends by an act of violence, when an organized group, the fire brigade, attacks Coalhouse Walker Jr. and destroys his car. Now group acting, motivated by collective passions and irrational drives, becomes the main factor of the narrative dynamics. The story of private, intimate bonds turns into a story of racial confrontation. The metamorphosis of Mother's Younger Brother is highly characteristic of this shift: humiliated in his devoted love, he cuts all family ties and becomes a zealous participant in the violent social conflict.

Members of the three families, the protagonists of the private stories of *Ragtime* are carefully selected as representatives of the main American social strata at the beginning of the twentieth century: the enterprising middle class, the struggling but ultimately successful new immigrants, and the awakening black Americans. Some prominent individual characteristics grow in these social and cultural conditions: Father's passion for exploration, Tateh's drive for advancement, Coalhouse Walker's ambition as a musician. The fictional characters are no less children of their time and culture than are the fictionalized persons.[11]

The set of fictionalized historical persons is impressive in its size and diversity. From the prominent characters J. P. Morgan, Houdini, Emma Goldman, Harry K. Thaw, Stanford White, and Evelyn Nesbit to the minor characters Teddy Roosevelt, Theodore Dreiser, Jacob Riis, Robert E. Peary, Henry Ford, Sigmund Freud, Thomas A. Edison, Scott Joplin, Booker T. Washington, and many others, the fictional world is crowded with agents who as financiers, industrialists, politicians, explorers and inventors, revolutionaries, architects, writers, journalists, scientists, and pioneers of jazz, popular culture, and cinema created twentieth-century America.[12] *Ragtime* is about a nation advancing rapidly toward maturity, pursuing vigorously its "manifest destiny."

The fusion of private and public acting that determines the narrative roles of fictional persons also determines those of fictionalized figures. Several fictional counterparts of the creators of twentieth-century America take part in highlighted private stories: the tragic love triangle involving White, Thaw, and Evelyn Nesbit, Houdini's attachment to his mother, Nesbit's affair with the Younger Brother. Some private stories, such as Roosevelt's African safari or Goldman's love affairs, are just tidbits, offered casually and haphazardly. A few fictionalized figures—Morgan, Ford, Edison—have no private story; this gap seems to indicate that their passionate involvement in public activities made their private lives irrelevant for Doctorow's fictional representation.

The second dimension of the fictional world of *Ragtime*, the domain of social groups and social action, is introduced as a grand tableau of New York at the dawn of the twentieth century, a city sharply divided into ghettolike ethnic and social areas.[13] Wave after wave of immigrants land in the harbor and are swallowed by the city: "Most of the immigrants came from Italy and Eastern Europe. . . . They went into the streets and were somehow absorbed in the tenements. They were despised by New Yorkers. They were filthy and illiterate. They stank of fish and garlic. They had running sores. They had no honor and worked for next to nothing. They stole. They drank. They raped their own daughters. They killed each other casually. Among those who despised them the most were the second-generation Irish, whose fathers had been guilty of the same crimes. Irish kids pulled the beards of old Jews and knocked them down. They upended the pushcarts of Italian peddlers" (13). The tone of the immigrant hater can be heard in this passage, but the worst conditions in the slums are constructed by a laconic impersonal narrative: "By the end of the month [of June] a serious heat wave had begun to kill infants all over the slums. The tenements glowed like furnaces and the tenants had no water to drink. The sink at the bottom of the stairs was dry. Fathers raced through the streets looking for ice. . . . Pillows were placed on the sidewalks. Families slept on stoops and in doorways. Horses collapsed and died in the streets" (17).

Popular culture is prominent in the social domain of *Ragtime*'s fictional world; in the not too distant future America will export this commodity to the whole world. By a metonymic transfer of the novel's title the entire age acquires the name of an early form of black American jazz. The spectacular tragic hero of the novel, Coalhouse Walker Jr., an excellent ragtime pianist, is an emblem of this age. Other forms of popular culture and entertainment, magic shows and baseball games, also make an appearance. But it is the surging popularity of moving pictures that will determine the cultural atmosphere of the twentieth century. Doctorow's narrative captures a crucial event of this triumphal rise, the birth of the star. Photographs and drawings of Evelyn Nesbit testifying at her husband's trial created "the first sex goddess in American history" (70). "Thus did Evelyn provide the inspiration for the concept of the movie star system and the model for every sex goddess from Theda Bara to Marilyn Monroe" (71).

American social life is ripe with violent conflicts, and Doctorow's fictional world is no idyll. A strike in the mills of the city of Lawrence, Massachusetts, leads to many violent incidents, culminating in a brutal police action against the strikers' children and wives (ch. 16). Police attacks on the meetings of the anarchists are routine (ch. 8). The most violent social conflict of the story, the occupation and the siege of the Morgan Library, is an act of war, what today would be called an act of terrorism, hitting the most elegant quarter of New York. It is simultaneously an episode of the perennial racial struggle in America and a tragic conclusion of the private story of Coalhouse Walker.[14] The novel starts as a suburban family idyll and ends as a tragedy with explosions in the centre of the city.

The structural affinities between the world of Schama's *Citizens* and the world of Doctorow's *Ragtime* that we observed in our semantic analysis do not override the general claim that in a historical world every entity, every person, every event has to be backed by documentary evidence. No such constraint shapes the fictional world of *Ragtime.* Its composition corresponds to our general postulate, namely, that historical-fiction worlds bring together fictional persons with historical counterparts (e.g., Sigmund Freud) and fictional persons without such counterparts (e.g., Coalhouse Walker). The story of *Ragtime* is a blend of events lifted from chronicles of the day (Robert White's murder) with those freely invented by the fiction maker (Coalhouse Walker's "uprising" and occupation of the Morgan Library). It is not surprising that *Ragtime* outraged mimetic critics who claim that historical fiction is not allowed to "distort" historical facts.[15]

Davis S. Gross called Doctorow "our most important historical novelist since World War II." Doctorow's "chief significance in the context of postmodern fiction," wrote Gross, was in "his invention of a certain form of the historical novel, . . . his eccentric bricolage—patching together, tinkering—with fragments, images of our real and imagined past" (1986, 339). I think that Gross offers here an answer not only to the question of Doctorow's significance in American letters but also, and more importantly, to the question what makes him a postmodern fiction writer. Doctorow is one of the most imaginative and free fabulators of the American postmodern, along with Kurt Vonnegut Jr. and John Barth. The main features of his fictional world are not absolutely new, but he uses them to create a maximally dense and broad world crowded with private and public persons, both fictional and fictionalized, characters whose relationships and fates develop in a random way and are stitched together at random into a nonlinear plot bordering on the absurd.[16] We are in the world of coincidences, severe contradictions, and unpredictable turns.[17] It is out of this chaotic and aleatory world that Doctorow's modern America emerges.

## 4. Fictional Quest for a Fictional Past: A. S. Byatt's *Possession: A Romance*

The subtitle of Byatt's *Possession: A Romance* is much more than a generic designation; it is a true indicator of the book's thematics and together with the epigraph from Nathaniel Hawthorne links Byatt's fiction to a rich and specifically English literary tradition. The epigraph from Hawthorne, despite its insistence on "laws" of art, stresses the freedom of the romance writer in contrast to the novelist. Hawthorne's historical romance *The House of the Seven Gables* connects "a bygone time with the very present that is flitting away from us."[18] And that is also Byatt's wager.

Kathleen Kelly calls *Possession* "a virtuoso postmodernist exercise that weaves together many strands: a contemporary story of academic conflicts, rivalries and discoveries; 19th-century chronicle of ill-fated love; and a meditation on the imagination and creativity" (1996, 78). There is a strong romantic strain in the double story of the book—the illicit love of two poets, the out-of-wedlock child, the sorry fate of the heroine, the nasty conflicts and intrigues of competing questors, even the digging up of a grave (quite in the tradition of Dickens's romance). The romantic strain coexists with a contrary literary tradition, the realistic fiction style.

A striking feature of Byatt's style is "thick" descriptions that provide the dense furnishing of the physical setting (in particular the interiors) of the fictional world. The proletarized intellectual Roland Michell, PhD, lives with his girlfriend, Val, in "a cavernous basement room" of a house in Putney with a "dark hall" and a window that "opened into a little yard with steps to the garden." Although their room was advertised as "a garden flat," they are not allowed to enter the garden. They have painted the room "apricot and white, to cheer it up; it was furnished with a double divan, two very old arm-chairs with curvaceous rolled arms and headrests, plum and plushy and dusty, a second-hand stained-oak office desk, where Roland worked, and a newer varnished beech desk, where the typewriter sat. . . . They have put up various posters; a British Museum poster from the Koran, intricate and geometric, a Tate advertisement for a Turner exhibition" (15).

When Roland and Maud Bailey penetrate the country mansion of the Baileys, they find another cavernous, although more spacious habitat. Step by step the inhabitants of the manor had been retreating into a smaller and smaller space, until the present generation ended up living in a servants' hall, "now superficially, and partially, converted for modern living." "At the end of this dim room was an open fireplace, in which a few huge logs still smouldered in a bed of white ash; on either side of this were two heavy, curved and padded armchairs, covered in velvet, a dark charcoal colour, patterned with dark purple flowers, a kind of glamorised fin-de-siècle bindweed. . . . The walls were whitewashed, and bore various pictures of horses, dogs and badgers, oils, watercolours, tinted photos, framed glossy prints." The impoverished English aristocracy lives as frugally as the unemployed intellectual, with the exception that there are treasures in the house preserved from the more glamorous past: there are the pictures on the walls (contrasting with Roland's cheap, probably free posters), and when tea is served it comes "in an exquisite Spode tea service, with a silver sugar bowl" (76–77).

These interiors seem to indicate that quite a few inhabitants of postmodern England were forced to retreat into caverns, some bearing the marks of the past imperial splendor, some simply contemporary slums. But let us not forget that the present is an era of contradictions. Dr. Maud Bailey's living room is extremely bright, furnished with refined taste in color and shape: "Maud's living room was not what might have been expected of a Victorian scholar. It was bright white, paint, lamps, and dining table; the carpet was a Berber off-white. The things in this room were brilliantly coloured in every colour, peacock, crimson, sunflower, deep rose, nothing pale or pastel. Alcoves beside the fireplace held a collection of spotlit glass, bottles, flasks, paperweights" (51). Not surprisingly, physically Maud (as seen by Roland) is a model of elegance: "she was dressed with unusual coherence for an academic" (38).

The styles of romance and of the realistic novel are two debts that the postmodern writer pays to the past. They contribute to the stylistic variety, typical of the postmodern fusion. Above, in section 2, I quoted Thiher to the effect that in a postmodern building one can discover the entire history of architecture. In Byatt's novel we discover the entire history of nineteenth- and twentieth-century English literature and literary criticism. The styles of romance and of literary realism are just a preview of what is to come. The features that deserve our close attention are those that make this work truly postmodern.[19]

The first of these features is a specific dyadic structure of the fictional world. The narrative of Byatt's novel weaves through two historically distant dimensions, the present postmodern time and the past Victorian period. This two-level world generates three stories: the story of the living, of the postmodern historians; the story of the dead, of the Victorian poets; and the story of the reconstruction of the life and work of the dead poets by the living questors. The stories of the living and of the dead run parallel—"they do neither cross nor blend," as Julija Rajneke notes (2002, 68)—but the epistemic quest provides a mutual mirroring of the cultural conditions and the individual fates of the postmoderns and of the Victorians. The understanding, empathy, identification across a century is possible because among the historians there are not only cool or calculating professionals but also, and primarily, devoted admirers of the dead poets. The parallel is especially eminent with regard to the main questors, Roland Michell and Maud Bailey. Their private relationship slowly and with difficulty begins to imitate the relationship of their "objects," the Victorian poets Randolph Henry Ash and Christabel LaMotte. Explicitly, and using the postmodern idiom masterfully, the text confirms this parallelism: "Somewhere in the locked-away letters, Ash has referred to the plot or fate which seemed to hold or drive the dead lovers. Roland thought, partly with precise postmodernist pleasure, and partly with a real element of superstitious dread, that he and Maud were being driven by a plot or fate that seemed, at least possibly, to be not their plot or fate but of those others. And it is probable that there is an element of superstitious dread in any self-referring, self-reflexive, inturned postmodernist mirror-game, or plot-coil that recognises that it has got out of hand, that connections proliferate apparently at random, that is to say with equal verisimilitude, apparently in response to some ferocious ordering principle, not controlled by conscious intention, which would of course, being a good postmodernist intention, require the aleatory, or the multivalent, or the 'free,' but structuring, but controlling, but driving, to some—to what?—end. Coherence and closure are deep human desires that are presently unfashionable. But they are always both frightening and enchantingly desirable" (421–22). I quote this reflection at length to demonstrate how stylistically authentic Byatt's postmodern interpretation of human acting and destiny is.

The epistemic quest for the literary past is carried out on an unprecedented scale. Literary history is no longer the vocation of insular loners locked for days in literary archives but a social activity carried out by teams and institutes, cooperating, competing, agreeing, arguing. And supported by grant funds. The reconstruction of the life and work of Randolph Henry Ash is pursued by two teams, one British, Professor Blackadder's London-based "Ash factory," the other American, Professor Cropper's research group based at a university in New Mexico. The British group includes the protagonist of the novel, Dr. Roland Michell, and Beatrice Nest; Nest is attached to the project by preparing an edition of the journal of Ash's wife. Professor Cropper is flush with money, while the British team is provided with rather modest means. Simultaneously and at first independently, a few English and American literary critics, particularly the second protagonist, Dr. Maud Bailey, are engaged in the study of the thus far neglected Victorian poetesse Christabel LaMotte. While the Ash scholars work with traditional historical and textual methods, the LaMotte students are feminists. The various incompatible approaches to the literary past and the arrogant ideological position of some individual researchers lead to different reconstructions of the past, to incompatible historical worlds. Ash is a classic of Victorian poetry for his admirers, but for the feminist Maud Bailey his work has no appeal: "All that cosmic masculinity. That nasty anti-feminist poem about the medium, what was it, Mummy Possest? All that ponderous obfuscation" (42). On the other hand, the "deconstructivist" Fergus Wolff makes only sarcastic comments on the excesses of feminist interpretations (34). The fictional critics join forces with counterparts of actual critics (Virginia Woolf, Swinburne) to create a cacophony of incompatible renderings of the past. In this respect, Byatt's construct of the epistemic quest for the past transcends literary history and provides a fictional model of contemporary historiography in general.[20]

The past emerges from dust and forgetting in fragments, like a jigsaw puzzle. The epistemic quest is a historiographic operation, a reconstruction of the past by the present (re)searchers. *Possession* is a genuine, pure exemplar of historiographic metafiction, a genre identified by Linda Hutcheon, but too broadly. The massive archival and editorial work undertaken by the competing teams has left no stone unturned. Summing up the records of Ash's private life, Professor Cropper states: "There is no record of any early peccadillo on Randolph's part, let alone any later one" (110). But suddenly and purely by accident Roland Michell finds a draft letter of Ash's, a trace of a mysterious, previously unknown friendship, maybe even a love affair. When the entire Ash-LaMotte correspondence is discovered, the true character of the relationship becomes clear.[21]

Byatt's romance is postmodern literature in its primary incarnation, a fictional game—interesting, surprising, ironic. It is a postmodern historical narrative on its own rather than the "engaged" postmodern created by ideologues. The special feature of Byatt's game is that the past itself—the lives and works of the two Victorian poet-protagonists—is a fictional construct.[22] It is certainly not uncommon to write fictional lives of famous poets and other cultural personalities, but Byatt's extraordinary achievement, the triumph of her creative powers, is that she herself composes the entire poetic *oeuvre* of the fictional Victorian poets.[23] This poetic creativity, this mastery of styles of "others," joins the romantic and the realistic styles to create the extraordinary stylistic variety of *Possession.*

Writing poetry and prose of fictional authors is the ultimate accomplishment of *poiesis*. Thanks to her extraordinary creative powers, Byatt is able to use a number of poetic styles to differentiate and individualize not only the writings of the two poets but also their poems of different genres and from different periods. Byatt is a writer of many voices: Byatt's plus Ash's plus LaMotte's, as well as many others'. She creates concrete, "authentic" texts that combine with other kinds of texts—literary criticism and history, letters, diaries, and so on—in an amazing textual collage.[24] In the last chapters of the book Byatt's own text almost disappears as she compiles an anthology of writings of several fictional authors and several genres: poems by Ash and LaMotte; LaMotte's prose fairy tales; Ellen Ash's journal and de Kercoz's "journal intime"; the Ash-LaMotte correspondence, letters from Fergus and Leonora, and a farewell note from Blanche Clover; excerpts from Cropper's monograph on Ash, Blackadder's note on an Ash poem, and other minor compositions. According to Chris Walsh, Byatt authors the writings of "no fewer than seventeen fictional characters" (qtd. in Gauthier 2006, 75). The freedom of the postmodern fiction writer to create, blend, and fuse numerous styles, literary and nonliterary, finds its ultimate expression in Byatt's textual collage.

Our analysis of Doctorow's *Ragtime* and Byatt's *Possession* reveals two common features of these postmodern historical fictions: diversity of styles and randomness in story development, or, rather, a loose combination of many stories. Postmodern historical fiction represents the past as a random, almost chaotic activity of both fictional persons and fictionalized counterparts of historical persons. The remarkable structural similarity between the fictional world of *Ragtime* and the historical world of Schama's *Citizens* does not imply dissolution of the boundary between historical fiction and history's reconstruction of the past. The blending of fictional and fictionalized persons in one fictional world and, in particular, Byatt's construction of a fictional past are reminders of the fiction writer's free imagination, which is denied the historian. The historical worlds of chapter III and the fictional worlds of chapter III and IV are clearly distinguished and do not allow fusions. The practice of postmodern historical fiction and postmodern history denies the equation postulated by the postmodern challenge.

# Counterfactual Narratives of the Past

We have noticed that some postmodern historical fictions not only deviate from commonly known historical facts but blatantly contradict them (IV.2). Now we will discover that the counterfactual representation of the past has deeper historical roots and broader motivations than the postmodern fictional experiments indicate. Why would anybody want to imagine what did not happen but might have happened? In this chapter I explore this weird phenomenon, assess how counterfactual representations could help us understand the past, and, primarily, determine how studying them could contribute to the illumination of the central problem of this book, the relationship between fiction and history.

## 1. Fundamentals of Counterfactual Thinking

Counterfactuals, counterfactual thinking, and counterfactual possible worlds have received much attention in the past two or three decades—in logic (Lewis 1973), in philosophy (Rescher 1973), and in certain fields of empirical enquiry, especially history (Ferguson, ed., 1997), political science (Tetlock and Belkin, eds., 1996), and social psychology (Roese and Olson, eds., 1995). Counterfactual thinking appears now as a significant part of human intelligence; it enriches reasoning by the ability of the imagination to construct nonactualized alternatives to what actually happened. Humans activate counterfactual thinking for many different reasons: to deal with negative affects arising from events or actions, to open new horizons for knowledge and understanding, to create narratives of alternative pasts, or simply to "catapult themselves beyond the muck and malignancy of the actual into the liberating realm of the possible" (Roese and Olson 1995b, 169). There are undeniably major differences in individuals' propensity for counterfactual thinking and in their preferences for certain kinds of counterfactuals (see Kasimatis and Wells 1995), but the capacity for this kind of thinking is obviously universal. Although the following example is taken from a fictional work, we could easily imagine a similar actual situation.

Mrs. Janet Carpenter was murdered Monday night. The Sunday before, she had gone for confession to Father Presteign. Commander Dalgliesh wanted to interrogate Mrs. Carpenter on Monday evening, but despite inspector Kate's objections, he put it off until the next morning. After the murder, the three fictional persons of P. D. James's novel *A Certain Justice* (1997) make the following comments "If that priest had told us on Sunday everything he knew, she'd still be alive" (Kate); "If we'd gone to interview her early Monday evening, she'd still be alive" (Dalgliesh); "If I had persuaded her to go to you immediately after she left the church, if I had insisted on accompanying her, she'd be alive today" (Father Presteign) (331). All these comments are counterfactual conditionals, expressing the perennial need of humans to ponder possible actions that might have prevented an actual event from happening or brought about a different actual event. Counterfactual thinking is invoked both in the mental stage antecedent to acting, that is, when the agents consider and assess available alternatives, and in the subsequent stage (as in our example), where counterfactuals serve to evaluate the outcome, soften its emotional impact, express regret, give praise or assign blame, and so on.

It is a proper task of psychology to study the various purposes, modes, and individual differences of counterfactual thinking in human praxis. One of the psychologists' tasks is to determine "psychological 'rules' that constrain people's considerations of which events or conditions to mentally mutate. We use the term counterfactual constraints to refer to these rules. . . . Counterfactual constraints serve the purpose of restricting all possible alternatives to a practical subset" (Seelau et al. 1995, 659–60). It is important to recognize that the psychologists are not talking about rules or prescriptions for "correct" counterfactual thinking but rather about observed regularities in this mental activity, often experimentally induced. And we have to bear in mind what the skeptics (Sherman and McConnell 1995) point out: counterfactual thinking, like any other mental procedure, can be highly biased, often dysfunctional, often leading to highly unreliable conclusions.

While the psychology of counterfactuals investigates their use in human life, the logic of counterfactual thinking strives for defining their formal structures and truth conditions. It is commonly accepted that the elementary counterfactual is a conditional statement of the form "If A had been true, then B would have been true." An example is, "If Hitler had won the war, Germans would have settled Eastern Europe." The past tense of the verb in the antecedent and the consequent differentiates the counterfactual conditional from conditionals expressing causal relationships, for example, "If it rains this afternoon, the match will be cancelled" (Woods 1997, 78). In this example the antecedent points to the future; since no fact has been established, the conditional is not a counterfactual statement. The best-known though not generally accepted logical formalism for counterfactuals was proposed by David Lewis (1973). It is based on the notion of possible worlds. Roughly speaking, counterfactual conditionals are true at some possible world different from the actual world. But even if we accept this general truth condition, we are not able to verify particular cases: "There simply is no way of verifying whether a counterfactual conditional statement is ever true" (Wright 1974, 50). Even Lewis admits the unreliability of his truth condition: "Some sensitive counterfactuals are so vague as to be unsuitable for use in serious discourse; . . . others have definite truth values only when context serves to narrow their range of vagueness; and . . . many more have quite definite truth values (in worlds of the sort we think we inhabit)" (1973, 94).

Some logicians (Rescher 1973; Adams 1975) have suggested that plausibility rather than truth value is the appropriate criterion for evaluating the counterfactuals' usefulness. They propose arranging counterfactuals on a scale defined by the degree of their probability in the actual world. The plausibility of counterfactuals is a continuous function between the values 1 (fully plausible) and 0 (implausible). A typology can be set up along this continuum. Its most significant points are as follows:

a. *Fully plausible counterfactuals (probability one) are confirmed by hard evidence from the actual world:* "If Oswald did not kill Kennedy, then someone else did" (example from Lewis 1973, 3). It is a historical fact that President Kennedy was killed. If the main suspect, Oswald, did not commit the crime, then somebody else did.

b. *Plausible counterfactuals (high probability) are confirmed by some evidence from the actual world:* "If Hitler had won the war, the Germans would have settled the Slavic East." Historical evidence of existing plans and experimental resettlements (see below, sec. 4) makes it highly probable that the Nazis would have pursued this course of action had they achieved victory in World War II.

c. *Implausible counterfactuals have a consequent that is highly improbable in the actual world:* "If Oswald did not kill Kennedy, somebody else would have" (example from Lewis 1973, 3). The idea that Kennedy's life had to end by his being killed is quite far-fetched. It is very likely that had he survived the Dallas *attentat,* he would have continued living until natural causes brought about his death.

d. *Totally implausible counterfactuals have a consequent of zero probability.* For our topic, the most typical case of this kind is anachronisms that violate the chronology of events: "If Napoleon had had a couple of tanks, he would have won the battle of Waterloo."

Let us note that in counterfactual thinking we quite often mutate just one event and consider the immediate possible consequences of this change. We can designate these constructs *short-term* counterfactual episodes. To be sure, possible long-term consequences can be considered, but these developments are just suggested, not constructed. Some theorists have distinguished between a counterfactual method that mutates just one factor and leaves other factors unchanged, the *ceteris paribus* method, and a systemic method that constructs total counterfactual worlds. Philip Tetlock and Aaron Belkin "see no easy resolution of the tension between the desire of methodologists to 'hold other things equal' and the insistence of latter-day Leibnizians that once we tamper with one element of the past, we have to trace through the causal implications for all other elements, in effect creating a full-fledged alternative world for each counterfactual." The authors advise choosing the method "on a case-by-case basis, with a minimum of metaphysical posturing. . . . In some cases, the grounds for suspecting systemic effects will be weak and the counterfactual exercise can approximate the austere parsimony of the thought experiment; in other cases, the grounds for suspecting systemic effects will be powerful and counterfactual exercises will acquire the narrative trappings of scenario generation, with detailed stories and subplots elaborated around why certain historical paths were not taken and what should have had to be different to activate them" (1996, 21).[1]

Before offering my own theoretical suggestions about the counterfactual constructions of the past, I find it necessary for the reader to get acquainted with this relatively little known kind of narrative. In the following two sections the reader will accumulate sufficient knowledge of the counterfactual narratives of the past, of their stories, their "heroes," and their historical settings. I must emphasize that the division into fictional and historical narratives is purely provisional, based primarily on the vocation of the writer and some paratextual markers.[2] In the final section we will learn that in the case of counterfactual constructions of the past the distinction between fictional and historical worlds is different than in the case of factual constructions: it requires a special theoretical consideration and brings revealing theoretical insights.

## 2. Counterfactual Fiction

Counterfactual stories of the past can be freely developed by fictional narratives, since there are no constraints imposed on the authors' imagination. Yet neither literary history nor literary theory paid much attention to this special subgenre of historical fiction until Edgar V. McKnight (1994) devoted his PhD dissertation to it. The dissertation is a solid survey of the history of the genre, beginning with its predecessors in the nineteenth century.[3] McKnight emphasizes that "it has fully emerged as a literary genre only since World War Two" (iii). Its thriving in the age of postmodernism is probably connected with the general undermining or erasing of established ontological boundaries characteristic of the postmodern imagination (McHale 1987, 10). Postmodern historical fiction generally cultivates ontological experiments in that it freely transforms entities of historical worlds into fictional entities (and vice versa) by playing with the category "historical fact" (see below, sec. 3.2). The chef-d'oeuvre of postmodern literature, Carlos Fuentes's *Terra Nostra* (1975), is, among other things, an "apocryphal counterhistory of the Spanish" (McHale 1987, 93), qualifying for the designation of counterfactual historical fiction. According to McHale, works like *Terra Nostra* are a parody of classic historical fiction; the historical past provides the actors and the stage for the "carnivalization" of history (90). This "Bakhtinian" interpretation neglects the more important features of counterfactual historical fiction, which link this fictional genre to counterfactual thinking in general.

Counterfactual fictional history is constructed as a global world of an alternative order, as a world in which the total conditions of social and individual acting are contrary to what we know about the corresponding actual world. The worlds of counterfactual historical fiction—unlike the worlds of science fiction—are contemporaneous with well-known historical worlds, and therefore the "distance" between the historical and the counterfactual world orders can be recognized. The social, political, and cultural order of the counterfactual world is imposed on the persons who live in that world and determines to a high degree their opportunities for, and their modes of, acting.

The prototype of this structure can be found in Ward Moore's novel *Bring the Jubilee,* published in 1953. Moore constructs a fictional world in which the North, after its calamitous defeat in the battle of Gettysburg, lost the "War of Southron Independence." The Peace of Richmond divided the country into the Confederacy and the "remaining" twenty-six United States. The punishment for defeat was impoverishment and a general stagnation of the United States, while the Confederacy (and some European states) thrived and made major technological progress. The story of the narrator-protagonist Hodgins McCormick Backmaker starts as an adventure story: he leaves his small hometown and goes to New York to seek a better existence. He is robbed, gets drawn into the activities of a terrorist organization (the Grand Army), witnesses a holdup, and rescues a young girl from vicious criminals. By sheer good luck he is chosen as a fellow of a private college-commune, Haggershaven, and after years of study becomes a widely published and well-known historian of the American Civil War. The protagonist's adventure story turns into science fiction when one of the fellows of Haggershaven invents a functioning time machine. Hodgins cannot resist the temptation and uses the machine to go back in time and witness the battle of Gettysburg. During his stay in the past, his most incredible adventure occurs: involuntarily he intervenes in the battle and changes its outcome. Thereby he changes not only the outcome of the war but the entire future. There is no Haggershaven in that future, so Hodgins cannot be brought back. He lives a life of servitude but witnesses the progress and expansion of the postbellum United States.

Ward Moore's novel was well received (McKnight 1994, 43), but it was overshadowed in the next decade by Philip K. Dick's *Man in the*

*High Castle* (1962). One reason for this novel's popularity might be that Dick was a successful science-fiction writer. After all, the connection between counterfactual historical fiction and science fiction embodied in Dick's *oeuvre* is not fortuitous. Science fiction projects a future that differs substantially from the actuality of the author's present; counterfactual historical fiction modifies the past to project a present that differs substantially from the actual state of affairs. A stronger reason for his novel's popularity is Dick's choice of a very topical, exciting counterfactual theme, the victory of Germany and Japan in World War II.

Dick's fictional world is set in the counterfactual United States, which the victorious Japanese and Germans have divided into three main parts. The eastern part, known as the United States of America, is a German protectorate. The western part, called the Pacific States of America, is a Japanese protectorate, of which San Francisco, the main setting of the novel, is a major business center. In between lie the Rocky Mountain States, relatively independent and enjoying a higher degree of freedom. Here, in Cheyenne, a writer by the name of Hawthorne Abendsen has written a novel strangely entitled *The Grasshopper Lies Heavy*. In it, the counterfactual world of *The Man in the High Castle* is reversed: Germany and Japan were defeated in World War II.[4] Abendsen's novel becomes an underground international bestseller and not surprisingly is prohibited in the German Reich.

In the political and social conditions of the counterfactual world, Dick creates an adventure story around two intrigues of high politics: the attempted assassination of Abendsen by a German agent and the German planning of a war against Japan. "Ordinary" fictional persons—Childan, a San Francisco antique dealer; Frank Frink, a Jewish refugee from the United States; and his ex-wife, Juliana—are drawn into the political adventure story. Their private stories—Frink's dubious efforts to establish himself in the new conditions, Childan's quest for social recognition and business success, and Juliana's unfortunate involvement with a German agent—are tokens of the lives of the defeated Americans.

The predominance of the political over the private story is also evident in a second fictional work that reverses the outcome of World War II, Robert Harris's *Fatherland* (1992). The story takes place in 1964, in a Greater German Reich, formed after the victory of Germany in World War II. The eastern enemy has been pushed behind the Urals and is unable to do more than harass German troops by guerrilla and terrorist attacks. Western Europe, including Great Britain, has been pacified and has formed a European Union under the German leadership. The two nuclear superpowers in the world, Germany and the United States of America, are locked in a cold war. On the eve of the celebrations of the Führer's seventy-fifth birthday, the Reich is preparing for the visit of the American president, Joseph P. Kennedy, which is expected to initiate a détente between the superpowers. At this point several mysterious deaths of former high Nazi officials occur in Berlin. The story of international politics turns into a detective story. Xavier March, the stubborn detective of the criminal police, although obstructed by the Gestapo, concludes that the deaths are connected to secret documents of the 1941 Wannsee Conference. At this conference, presided over by Reinhardt Heydrich, plans for the Final Solution were drawn up. A visiting American journalist, Charlotte Maguire, becomes involved not only in March's investigation but also in his life. The ending is underdetermined: "Charlie" is on her way to neutral Switzerland with the documents of the Wannsee Conference, but it is only through March's belief that the success of her mission is authenticated. March himself, surrounded by pursuers, draws his gun either to engage in a hopeless fight or to commit suicide.

The cast of characters of Harris's novel is typical of historical fiction: a mix of persons with and without historical counterparts. The fictional persons survive their historical counterparts: Hitler and Goebbels did not commit suicide in 1945, and Heydrich recovered from his wounds suffered in the 1943 assassination attempt in Prague. These leaders remain in the background of the story, although they obviously pull the strings. The perpetrators and victims of the "purge," less prominent Nazi functionaries, also defy the fate of their historical counterparts: one of the victims, Josef Buhler, was not executed in Poland in 1948, and one of the villains, the cruel Gestapo general and March's main opponent, Globocnik, did not commit suicide in 1945.[5] The coexistence and interaction of fictional and fictionalized characters is the main proof that the world of counterfactual historical fiction displays the same overall structure as the world of standard historical fiction.

Attractive as it may be, the reversal of the outcome of World War II is not the sole triggering event of recent counterfactual fiction. The prominent and versatile British author Kingsley Amis chooses quite a different counterfactual historical event to construct an alternative present world. The action of *The Alteration* is set in 1976 (the year of the novel's publication), but its England is much different from the actual one of that year. There is no Elisabeth II, no democracy, no technological progress. The country is a clericalist-fascist tyranny with its empire intact but its sovereignty severely restricted. The highest ruler of England, indeed of all Europe, is the pope, residing in Rome. This counterfactual present is the consequence of the holy victory of the Catholic side in an unspecified religious war.

The totalitarian rule hampers any progress, whether social or technological. The laws, the social customs, and the overall social atmosphere of this England are strongly reminiscent of the Middle Ages. One archaic custom that survives into 1976 is the castrating of talented boy singers. Focusing on his hero, the wunderkind singer Hubert Anvil, Amis writes an adventure story of his attempt to escape his fate. Along the way, Hubert is helped by the ambassador of New England, an independent and relatively free nation. Hubert succeeds in boarding an airship bound for New England, but just before departure, suffering from an illness that requires the very operation he was trying to avoid, he has to be carried ashore.

My set of counterfactual historical novels is highly selective but representative enough to allow us to formulate a few general conclusions about the structure of the genre's fictional world:

The fictional world deviates from the historical world because at some point in the near or distant past an event contrary to well-attested historical facts occurred: the victory of the Catholic side in the European holy war, the victory of the South in the American Civil War, the victory of the Axis in World War II.

The fictional world is characterized by a social and political order that is substantially different from the order of the corresponding historical world: an impoverished and decaying United States, medieval totalitarianism in England, fascist domination of Europe and the United States.

The fictional world is furnished with objects that are not found in the actual historical world: Amis's super-train, running at 195 miles per hour and crossing the Channel on a bridge 23 miles long (an exception to the general technological backwardness of the counterfactual England), Moore's minibiles and tinugraphs, and others. At the same time, many objects of the corresponding actual world are missing in the counterfactual world, such as airplanes and sound recorders in Amis's *Alteration.*

The movers of the counterfactual historical world are political, military, religious, and other leaders, personalities with or without historical counterparts. Writers of counterfactual historical fiction alter not only the global structure of the historical world but also the life histories and individuating properties of historical persons. We have noticed the altered life histories of the leaders of the German Reich in Harris's *Fatherland.* In *Bring the Jubilee* Henry Adams is an unorthodox historian criticizing "the Bostonian essayists" William and Henry James (36), George B. Shaw is "an obscure Irish theologian" (38), and Carl Jung is a "Swiss police chief" (41). Kingsley Amis turns Jean-Paul Sartre into a French Jesuit who writes commentaries on medieval tracts and Edgar Allan Poe into a "brilliant young general" who perishes at the moment of his military triumph in the war of 1848–50; Amis's Mozart writes a second Requiem (K. 878), and William Walton composes religious music. All these seemingly banal transformations serve one significant purpose: to reveal the link between counterfactual historical imagination and possible worlds. Every person could have existed in other worlds, could have led a different life from the one he or she lived. By performing these transformations *en masse,* counterfactual historical fiction shows its ability to take readers to many possible worlds.

Within the world that they inhabit, "ordinary" fictional characters play out adventure stories, detective stories, science-fiction stories. This feature links counterfactual historical fiction closely to popular literature; indeed, it may make it one of popular fiction's genres. Still missing are counterfactual fictions comparable to the major works of historical fiction. Counterfactual historical fiction has had its Walter Scott but still awaits its Lev Tolstoy and Gustave Flaubert.

In all the works cited the principal paradox of counterfactual historical fiction is apparent: while the counterfactual world demonstrates the contingency of social, military, and political history, the life histories of the persons acting in this world are predetermined by traditional fabulas. The stories they enact are not different from those typical of standard fiction—stories of personal relationships, struggles, quests. The most prominent of these narrative schemas is the story of the rebel—Hodgins Backwater, Xavier March—and his failure. The most tragic failure befalls the rebels in Amis's totalitarian world: the dissident priest Lyall is brutally killed by the order's guardians, and in Hubert's case nature itself intervenes to prevent his escape from the predetermined fate.

## 3. Counterfactual History

David Lewis argued (1973, 75–76) that in a world governed by deterministic laws it would take a "miracle" to bring about a counterfactual state of affairs. But the world of human acting, of human history, is not deterministic.[6] In fact, any complete description of change has to take into account the contingency of human acting: "In the concept of an action," writes the founder of the modern theory of action, "is . . . implicit a comparison or contrast between a state of affairs resulting from the action and another state which would otherwise, i.e. had it not been for the performance of the action, have obtained. . . . That which 'would otherwise have obtained' never comes true (occurs). It is 'contrary to fact'" (Wright 1974, 41). Actual human history drags counterfactual history along as its shadow. A comprehensive reconstruction of the past has to include the construction of alternative, counterfactual, nonactualized strains.

In order to introduce the main "genre" of the counterfactual construction of the past, I shall resort again to a fictional work, albeit one very different from a popular mystery novel: the philosophical tale "Sanatorium under the Sign of the Hourglass" (1937), written by the Polish surrealist Bruno Schulz. The narrator-protagonist visits the surreal sanatorium to find his father, who had died in the actual world, alive and well. Dr. Gotard explains to the narrator that such a counterfactual event can be effected by a special manipulation of time: "Here we reactivate the past with all its possibilities" (117). This is a precise description of what the so-called counterfactual or alternative history does: it reactivates the past with its preactualized possibilities and then considers how human history might have proceeded after a counterfactual possibility had been actualized.

It is interesting that André Maurois narrated a similar story in "If Louis XVI Had Had an Atom of Firmness," his contribution to J. C. Squire's *If It Had Happened Otherwise* ([1932] 1972). Maurois's contribution is an impossible text, a "text after death" (see Doležel 1998, 159), a narrative of the posthumous experience of a historian who is admitted to the "Archives of Unrealized Possibilities." Indeed, only in the posthumous (i.e., supernatural) world can a person gain access to the complete history of the world, which includes not only the actual past but also all the nonactualized alternatives.[7]

Let us stay for a moment with the Squire collection, which shows us very clearly how counterfactual history was originally practiced. Squire assembled an international pleiad of prominent men of letters of the time "to re-examine and re-value great moments of history" ([1932] 1972, xiii). Squire's team cultivated counterfactual history as a game of wit, intellect, and, primarily, imagination. A strong imagination was necessary because the projections of the future after the counterfactual turn were so daring and far-reaching that only an active imagination could construct them. We can call this counterfactual history a history of *longue durée:* its alternative world usually spans centuries.

Philip Guedalla, for example, pinpoints the battle of Lanjerón (1491) as a turning point in the history of Europe and the whole world and then considers the consequences of a counterfactual victory of the Moors. The kingdom of Granada becomes a European power in the twentieth century. In Guedalla's counterfactual construct the historical blends with the fictional: the factual Spanish discoveries and colonization of South America ([1932] 1972, 4) are as much part of his history as the imaginary zenith of the kingdom of Granada at the end of the seventeenth and beginning of the eighteenth century (9–10). In the same vein, historical figures (persons with historical counterparts) coexist and interact with fictional persons—the historical Louis XIV and the fictional kings of Granada, Abdalla I and Boabdil IV. A telling example of pure fiction making is the episode of Benjamin Franklin's visit to Granada: "A delegation from Philadelphia, headed by Benjamin Franklin himself, found a chilly welcome in Granada and was abruptly dismissed from the royal presence with bland expressions of regret that, after an exhaustive search, no reference could be discovered in the Koran to any land beyond the Pillars of Hercules, and that in consequence the Captain of the Faithful could hardly be expected to associate himself with the inhabitants, however deserving, of lands that in his belief did not exist. The angry expostulations of Franklin produced no effect, and his subsequent offer to provide the Alhambra with lightning-conductors was regarded as the best proof of his connection with the powers of darkness" (12–13).

Clearly, a satirical tone can be heard here, a symptom of the literariness of Guedalla's text.

Hilaire Belloc's story makes a banal, accidental event the turning point of history. The assumption that triggers the counterfactual version of the well-known Varenne episode of the French Revolution is that Drouet's cart got stuck and thus he could not block the carriage in which Louis XVI was fleeing the revolutionary upheaval. Consequently, the king and his family were able to escape to the loyal Rhine army. The topsy-turvy history then continues when the royalist forces (under Lafayette!) defeat the rebels in the battle at Valmy. This victory ensures the survival of the Bourbon monarchy and the deletion of Napoleon from history. In a feast of free imagination, Belloc's counterfactual history is led up to the present (1928).

The mix of fictionalized historical agents and fictional persons—a feature of historical fiction—is also characteristic of H. A. L. Fisher's narrative. The author develops a counterfactual history from the popular legend that Napoleon did not die at Santa Helena but escaped to America. Fisher's Napoleon interacts as easily with historical persons, such as Madame Walewska, Jefferson, Webster, and Bolivar, as he does with fictional creations, such as the unnamed narrator, the narrator's uncle George, and the New York jeweler Van Byl.

A more plausible historical alternative is considered in the contribution written by Emil Ludwig, a prominent German writer and biographer. Entitled "If the Emperor Frederick Had Not Had Cancer," it projects a counterfactual world whose triggering event is the assumption that the German emperor Frederick III would have been allowed to reign to the fullness of his time instead of just four months. Ludwig's world reflects actual history in two respects: only counterparts of historical personalities (Bismarck, Frederick III, his wife Victoria, William II, Queen Victoria) are agents of the story; and these persons bear traits vouchsafed by history. They act out a counterfactual history of *courte durée* in a world that is determined by the parameters of the actual historical world. Concentrating on domestic reforms and international alliances, Frederick wants to build a Germany that is prosperous, progressive, and at peace with its neighbors and old enemies. In this counterfactual world August 1, 1914, marks, not the beginning of World War I, but the regrettable passing of "this wise prince" ([1932] 1972, 248).

The historical character of Ludwig's alternative world is certainly reinforced by the narrative mode of his text; it is the "objective," authoritative third person, typical of historical narrative. However, the majority of texts in Squire's volume borrow their narrative modes from literary narrative. The case of the stylistic collage is especially telling: it is inspired by the "narrative symposium" (multimodal narrative) of modern fiction (see Doležel 1973, 112–14). Guedalla's collage interweaves historical writing, a travel guide, and various historical "documents"—private correspondence, a House of Commons record, newspaper articles. A similar mix of diverse discourses is employed in the construction of Belloc's counterfactual world. Fisher's contribution is an *Ich*-form narrative related by a witness of Napoleon's landing in Louisiana. The witness becomes a participant in the counterfactual events when he serves as Napoleon's translator and interpreter. Maurois's contribution is, as already mentioned, a radical experiment, "text after death," an *Ich*-narrative of the posthumous experience of a historian.

Overall, we have to conclude that the counterfactual constructs of Squire's collection are fictional worlds structurally and semantically equivalent to the worlds of historical fiction. While purporting to be thought experiments in historical study, they are in fact fictional narratives. The fictional worlds called forth by the authors' imagination are hardly of any cognitive significance. Guedalla's projection, for instance, certainly highlights the historical significance of the battle of Lanjerón, but there is no reason why his counterfactual scenario could not over the centuries provide alternatives that would have prevented the rise of the kingdom of Granada. Purely imaginary counterfactual scenarios cannot escape the banality of the ultimate counterfactual: "If Columbus did not discover America, somebody else would have."

Purely imaginary counterfactual histories in the spirit of the Squire collection blossom in the postmodern era (see, e.g., Cowley, ed., 2003). Their method of constructing a counterfactual world of the past is relatively simple: take counterparts of historical persons and get them involved in nonactual, undocumented, imaginary political and/or military actions. Although these counterfactual histories might be rather popular, their cognitive gain is nil.

It is probably the counterfactual history of the Squire type that is responsible for the fact that the majority of practicing and theoretical historians have been skeptical about counterfactual histories for epistemological reasons. Johannes Bulhof summarizes the objections of those who see in counterfactual "speculations" about the past just a "parlor game" (Carr 1964, 44): "We simply have no way of knowing, no way of justifying beliefs about what might have happened. . . . The merely possible is not something we can test, and it is not something we can use the techniques of historians to analyze" (Bulhof 1999, 145). Bulhof himself does not share this skepticism and points to three crucial tasks of historians in which counterfactual thinking is indispensable and practiced (sometimes implicitly): ascribing causality, evaluating historical figures' actions, and judging the importance of historical events. He also assembled a collection of counterfactual assumptions made by historians. I quote from him Daniel Goldhagen's reflections on why Hitler chose to exterminate the Jews. It had been suggested that one possible motivation was that no country was willing to accept a massive Jewish emigration from occupied Poland and the Soviet Union. The second explanation was just Hitler's bad moods. Goldhagen disagrees with these arguments, resorting to counterfactual thinking: "This argument implies, counterfactually, that had these putative motivation-engendering circumstances not been brought about—had Hitler's allegedly volatile moods not allegedly swung, had the Germans been able to 'resettle' millions of Jews—then Hitler and others would have preferred some other 'solution' and then millions of additional Jews would have survived the war. This counterfactual reasoning is highly implausible" (Goldhagen 1996 424; qtd. in Bulhof 1999, 149). It is noteworthy that Goldhagen rejects putative motivations of the Holocaust on the basis that counterfactual alternatives are "highly implausible."

Many prominent historians have rejected the skepticism regarding counterfactual history and made valuable contributions to its "legalization." Often quoted is Tacitus's suggestion that the history of the Roman Empire would have been quite different if Germanicus had not died so prematurely: "Had he been the sole arbiter of events, had he held the powers and title of King, he would have outstripped Alexander in military fame as far as he surpassed him in gentleness, in self-command and in other noble qualities." Almost two thousand years later the meticulous historian of World War I David Stevenson claimed that the war had not been inevitable, that alternative courses of political action had been available in 1914: "Although the Austrians were exacerbated with Serbia, they greatly overestimated the threat it posed to them, and to have accepted its qualified acquiescence in their ultimatum would have been a more than adequate response to the challenge that the Sarajevo assassinations undoubtedly posed.... As for the Germans,... provided [they] maintained adequate land and naval defense forces, there was no risk to their territory, and alternatives to war as a solution to their predicament had not been exhausted. But the quality of decision-making in Berlin was execrable" (2004, 484). Winston Churchill, who, as we shall see, had some experience in constructing counterfactual history, wrote in his war memoirs: "I have often wondered . . . what would have happened if two hundred thousand German storm troops had actually established themselves ashore. The massacre would have been on both sides grim and great. There would have been neither mercy nor quarter. They would have used terror and we were prepared to go all lengths" (1949, 279). The prominent war historian John Keegan entered the controversy about the timing of the cross-Channel invasion in World War II by skillfully combining factual statements with counterfactual suppositions: "A cross-Channel invasion staged in 1943 would have to be prepared in 1942. In that year, the battle of the Atlantic had not been won, the strategic-bombing offensive against German cities was only beginning, the base for a great American army in Britain had not been built, the landing fleet was still under construction, and so on. Germany may well have been less ready to withstand an Allied cross-Channel invasion in 1943 than it proved to be in 1944, but Britain and America were less ready to mount it. The controversy seems pointless" (1995, 22).

In these and similar cases the historian's thought experiment helps to assess the significance of a historical event.[8] Because the past is unchangeable, because history is a single-run process, we cannot experiment with it as we can with regularly repeated phenomena; the historian resorts to the common human faculty of counterfactual thinking and alters the past in his head, by his imagination. It was Fernand Braudel, one of the founding members of the influential Annales school, who posited this cognitive role of counterfactual constructs: "It may be a bad habit to rewrite history as it never was, to alter the course of major events so as to imagine what might have happened. But although a sleight-of-hand like this may be an illusion, it is not pointless. In its own way, it measures the weight of events, episodes and actors who were believed, or believed themselves, to be responsible for the entire course of history." Braudel singles out one decisive moment in the history of France, the reign of François I: "If one could begin history all over again, as one can an experiment in a laboratory, what food for thought there would be in a France embracing Protestantism without a war, almost amicably, at the whim of a king. After a volte-face of this order, the history of France would have been completely different, and with it the history of Europe as a whole" (1980, 73, 75). Similarly, the prominent English historian Hugh Trevor-Roper in an essay aptly titled "History and Imagination" asserts the significance of unrealized alternatives for historical explanation: "At any given moment in history there are real alternatives, and to dismiss them as unreal because they were not realized . . . is to take the reality out of the situation. How can we 'explain what happened and why' if we only look at what happened and never consider the alternatives, the total pattern of forces whose pressure created the event?" Trevor-Roper takes as his prime example the critical moment of World War II when, after the defeat of France, England stood alone against Hitler: "I do not hesitate to say that in 1940–41 a mere accident, and one which might easily have occurred, could not only have reversed the outcome of the war, and transformed the subsequent shape of the world, but also have imposed upon the world a new synthesis of ideas and power, creating a new context for both politics and thought" (1980, 12–13, 11).

The need to consider counterfactuals in historical explanation has also been emphasized by philosophers. Geoffrey Hawthorn, expanding on Robert Nozick's idea, provides an enlightening summation:

> It [counterfactual reasoning] promises that kind of understanding, as Nozick describes it, which comes from locating an actual in a space of possibles, showing "the connections it would have to other non-actual things"; the kinds of understanding we gain, for instance, when we see how possible, even probable, other lines of species evolution were at some distant point in the past, and realize how improbable our own has been; when, in considering the success of Europe since the end of the fifteenth century, we realize that a reformed Christianity might not have been essential to it, or Islam inimical; when, in seeing how powerful a Confederate nation-state would have been at

> a moment when the extension of democracy and lower-class rights more generally, even in the United States, was by no means assured, we realize how what we now think of as "progress" was by no means assured; when, in considering the fate of social democracy elsewhere in northern and western Europe since the 1950s, we see more clearly what did not happen in Britain and why; when, in reflecting on our own lives, we see how else we might have lived them. (1991, 17–18)

These pronouncements imply that counterfactual thinking provides strong arguments against historical determinism, against the Hegelian claim that history follows some transcendent "laws." The course of history is not predictable, because history is the acting and interacting of human individuals and groups with all their random factors: conflicts of intentions and interests, impulses of passions and drives, accidents, errors of judgment, and even sheer good or bad luck.

As already mentioned, the conception of history as contingent is in full accord with the modern philosophy of human acting proposed by its founder, Georg H. von Wright. Von Wright emphasized that in every situation humans have a choice between alternative actions, the bottom line being the choice between doing something and doing nothing. In order to know an agent's life history "we must know not only how the world actually changes, but also how it would have changed from one occasion to the next, had it not been for the agent" (1968, 43–44, 47). Human history is a massive complex of private and social actions and interactions carried out by numerous persons-agents. All the snarls and bends, all attempts, successes, and failures constituting the unavoidable contingency of acting, are deposited in history. Considering nonactualized possibilities also reveals that even at such moments when the fate of entire countries or empires is at stake, random factors might decide the outcome. Would the October Revolution have succeeded "if by chance Lenin had been killed in the summer of 1917?" asks Irving Howe, returning to Leon Trotsky's question. And he adds that Trotsky's answer was "a gingerly no, it probably would not have succeeded, so central was the role of this individual" (1978, 16). But if the October Revolution had not succeeded, the twentieth-century history of Russia and of the entire world would have been radically different. Gavriel Rosenfeld, who concentrates on the three most popular "themes" of North American counterhistories—

"The Nazis win World War II," "The South wins the Civil War," and "The American revolution does not take place"—considers alternative history "inherently presentist. It explores the past less for its own sake than to utilize it instrumentally to comment upon the present. Based as it is upon conjecture, alternate history necessarily reflects its authors' hopes and fears" (2002, 93). From his study of the three counterfactual themes he concludes: "At least in the American context, alternate histories have shifted their representations of a given historical topic in accordance with the mood of the era. Periods of time perceived as ascendant have tended to elicit allohistories that validate the present by imagining an inferior past, while eras thought to be in decline have tended to elicit allohistories that criticize the present by imagining the past as superior in any number of ways" (103). Rosenfeld believes that evidence from other nations will confirm this thesis, but I believe that even his American evidence is rather meager and his thesis unconvincing.

The idea of the contingency of history and the idea of the need to construct historical worlds as multidimensional models are the two most significant theoretical achievements of counterfactual thinking in historiography. In this book on fiction and history we are, however, also concerned with alternative histories as parts or aspects of the representations of concrete, particular events or episodes of the past. In their cognitive function counterfactual events or episodes are, to use Daniel Kahneman's formulation, "mental simulations," "a form of elaborative thinking in which one imagines the unfolding of a sequence of events, from an initial counterfactual starting point to some outcome" (1995, 378). It was Alexander Demandt who initiated a theory of counterfactual history as "mental simulation." He started by weighing carefully the role of chance in history, suggesting that its force varies depending on the stage of the historical process and on the "sector" of history. In a vivid metaphor Demandt shows that "numerous historical processes have a funnel structure. They begin with a wide-open situation, where all kinds of things are still possible, but become narrowed in the course of time and gain in speed in the same measure as they lose in freedom. . . . Then in the final stage it becomes tempting to look back on the chance events which made the whole thing possible or could have prevented it." As far as the "sectors" of history are concerned, Demandt believes that the force of chance is in inverse proportion to the role personalities play in the historical process; it is very strong in the history of art, literature, and religion but relatively weak in the history of science and technology (1993, 69–113, 27, 26–34).

Demandt was the first counterfactual historian to realize that some restrictions must be imposed on counterfactual "mental simulations." He specified two such restrictions or selective criteria:

> One is that the different outcomes should lie within the narrower domain of the conceivable; the other is that as much as possible should depend on it. This means those cases in which far-reaching decisions hung on a knife's edge. Comparatively uninteresting and heuristically unproductive are speculations about unrealized alternatives which while they open up far-reaching perspectives are nonetheless highly improbable. . . . It is equally uninviting to reflect upon alternatives which could easily have happened differently but would have had little effect on the course of the events. What would have happened if, for example, Nero had succeeded in fleeing from Rome in 68, Louis XVI from France in 1792, Napoleon to America in 1815, or Mussolini to Switzerland in 1945 is comparatively uninteresting. All of these people were finished. (1993, 69–70)

I have quoted Demandt quite extensively because so far, to my knowledge, it has not been appreciated that he initiated a *critique* of counterfactual alternatives, refusing as useless some of the very popular cases.

Applying the criteria of significance and richness of consequences, Demandt analyzed fifteen counterfactual episodes (adding a few possible candidates). Typical of his method is the construction of the alternative "If Pontius Pilate has pardoned Jesus in A.D. 33?" (89–94). Let us observe briefly Demandt's method. First, he distinguishes three kinds of consequences of the counterfactual and spells out the most likely for each kind:

1. The consequences for Jesus's personal life: he probably "would have turned bourgeois, married Mary Magdalene, and ended his life as a peaceful carpenter in Nazareth" (91).

2. The consequences for the Christian religion: "the Crucifixion sets its mark so strongly on early Christian thought that its removal would have meant the disappearance of the religion" (91). But the need for a

new religion was so strong that Christianity would have been replaced by one of the religions that lost in competition with it, most likely the "solar Mithras cult" (92).

3. The consequences for the Roman Empire: "If Christianization did not take place, the empire might even have survived."

At this point Demandt constructs a counterfactual history of *longue durée:* "If we postulate the pardoning of Jesus, we find ourselves in a medieval period whose cities are built not around churches and cathedrals but around sun temples and capitols; in which not the Bible but Homer, Virgil, and the *Edda* are read; in which there are no religious wars and no Inquisition but also no hospitals and no poor relief" (93).

Demandt's counterfactual projections can certainly be contested, especially his *longue durée* vision, but at least they are definite enough to allow contesting. Moreover, they are based on pieces of historical evidence and on opinions of some predecessors: Ernest Renan on the sun cult, Voltaire and Gibbon on the import of Christianity on the collapse of the Roman Empire. Demandt's claim that "even neglected possibilities can to a certain extent be reasoned about by the use of evidence" confirms our conviction that his work marks the beginning of a new era in counterfactual thinking about the past, an era in which counterfactual history looks more and more like an integral part of historiography. Let us contemplate the theoretical foundations on which this new phase could advance.

## 4. Fictional Worlds Fit for History

In the first section of this chapter I presented a sample of counterfactual narratives that proclaimed their fictional character by both structural and pragmatic symptoms. These narratives are a special subgenre of historical fiction, and their worlds are fictional in the standard sense.[9] But the counterfactual representations presented in section 3 are of a different origin and purpose: they are constructed by historians, and their aim is to contribute to a better understanding of the past by joining counterfactual and "factual" worlds in a multidimensional representation of the past. A fundamental question arises: what kind of possible worlds are these counterfactual representations?

In answering the question let me first point to a structural distinction: we have seen that counterfactual historical fictions construct worlds that include both the domain of social (public) acting and the domain of private (individual) acting. In contrast, historians delete or minimize the domain of private acting in the counterfactual world. They focus on modulating significant (global) social, political, economic, or military historical conditions. For counterfactual history, the individual is interesting only as a "leader" of social, historically relevant acting or as an occasional agent of historically significant events. Let us recall the fate of Drouet in Hilaire Belloc's counterfactual history (1932): when he fails in his historical mission, he disappears from Belloc's world.

However, the common feature of the two kinds of counterfactual constructs is more significant and theoretically challenging. *All worlds of counterfactual history, whether constructed by historians or by fiction makers, whether their function is cognitive or aesthetic, are semantically fictional.* This radical claim, which as far as I know is here made for the first time, is supported primarily by the fact that no counterfactual worlds are models of the past; they cannot be models of anything, because the counterfactual past never existed. The construction of the world of counterfactual history begins with a statement that is false in the actual world, such as "Germany won World War II." As we already know from Georg von Wright, we can ask whether the counterfactual statement is more or less likely, more or less plausible, but it can only be false. The theoretical import of this thesis is far-reaching: the falseness of counterfactual statements about the past presupposes the existence of factual, that is, true, statements about the past, such as "Germany lost World War II." If there were no historical facts, there would be no historical counterfacts.

The truth value of a counterfactual statement about the past changes radically if a (logical) statement has the form of a (verbal) sentence in a text constructing a fictional world. It has been convincingly demonstrated in fictional semantics that sentences of world-constructing texts are neither true nor false (see Pavel 1986; Doležel 1998; and II.4 in this volume). The specific case of texts constructing counterfactual history confirms this theorem of the logic of fiction, first proclaimed by Gottlob Frege. There is no counterfactual world preexisting the constructing text; the world is constructed online by the progressing text. Just as Flaubert was free to let Emma Bovary die of self-inflicted poisoning, of old age, or any of a number of kinds of death, so the writers of counterfactual history are free to let World War II end in the victory of the Axis, in the Red Army's overrunning the whole of Europe, in the defeat of England, in the United States' concluding a separate peace agreement with the Axis powers. And they can continue building a counterfactual world in any shape or direction that their imagination proposes, since no truth conditions are imposed on their writing.

Let me present a radical case of the "arbitrariness" of the online construction of a counterfactual world of the past by returning for a moment to the Squire collection ([1932] 1972). We find here a special kind of parody, the self-parody of counterfactual history. The effect is created when the counterfactual event is taken as a historical fact and its converse is taken as a nonactualized possible. The method is demonstrated in Belloc's contribution when the "historian" Mr. Clarke considers the following possibility: "I have always thought that if Drouet could have pulled that cart out in time, could have blocked the passage, halted the coach and so had time to rouse the Mayor of Varenne and so to effect his purpose, the whole story of Europe might have been changed" (83–84). A fully developed self-parody is Winston Churchill's witty essay considering the "counterfactual" "If Lee Had Not Won the Battle of Gettysburg." According to Churchill, the negation of the counterfactual did not lead to what we know as the actual history of the United States after the Civil War. Churchill's history continues in the counterfactual stream: the nation is divided into the South and the North, facing each other in hostility and engaged in an arms race. But all ends well with the formation in 1905 of the "English-speaking Association" (191). The association was a powerful force for peace in the entire world. It prevented World War I and stimulated the European governments to start negotiations toward "An United States of Europe." Churchill's anti-history ends at the time of his writing (1932), with no Hitler in sight! This parody of counterfactual history is the ultimate proof of the freedom of the counterfactual historian's imagination.[10]

If we claim that all counterfactual constructions of the past are fictional worlds, do we contradict those historians who claim that counterfactual narratives can enhance our knowledge and deepen our understanding of the past? To answer this question we have to consider a more general problem: do fictions provide knowledge, and if so, under what conditions? There are theorists of fiction, adherents of the mimetic doctrine, who claim that fictions are (more or less faithful) representations of the actual world (see Doležel 1998) and that as such, they convey knowledge about human affairs, the human psyche, human history. Some popular versions of mimeticism, especially journalistic or pedagogic versions, consider fictions primarily a source of knowledge and show the readers what they can learn from reading (or watching) fictional works. Historical-fiction narratives have been especially widely touted as sources of knowledge. It has been claimed that the best and most fascinating account of Napoleon's invasion of Russia in 1812 is Leo Tolstoy's *War and Peace,* despite Shklovsky's demonstration ([1928] 1970) that the novel canonizes a legend. Naïve readers often fall for this bait, but historians have consistently warned, and been warned, against using historical fiction as a source of knowledge about the past (see IV.1). The method of fictional-world making cannot provide testable representations of the actual world, whether in its present or in its past state.

So how does a historian proceed if he or she proposes to construct a counterfactual world that, despite its fictional character, would provide knowledge about the past? For an answer to this question we shall go to Niall Ferguson's collection (Ferguson, ed., 1997), the foundational work of the new conception of counterfactual history. Ferguson and his contributors show that in order to obtain cognitive gains from fictional worlds of alternative history, their construction has to submit to certain constraints.[11] These constraints correspond to, or are derived from, the standard principles of historical-knowledge acquisition: the construction of the fictional counterfactual worlds has to approximate as closely as possible the procedures of historical-worlds construction. Fergusonian counterfactual historians tame fictionality; they fashion counterfactual fictional worlds into shapes or structures that promote their cognitive value.

Niall Ferguson's new theoretical base of alternative history is provided by an explicitly formulated set of restrictions.[12] The first task of the counterfactual historian is to decide "which counterfactual questions to pose," that is, which of the innumerable nonactualized counterfactual courses of history to chose for his mental experiment. The selection is guided by three criteria:[13]

1. The counterfactual has to be "plausible," "probable," or "credible" (see above, sec. 1). "For example, no sensible person wishes to know what would have happened in 1848 if the entire population of Paris sprouted wings, as this is not a plausible scenario." All anachronisms have to be rejected, because they are implausible. There is no cognitive gain in considering the possibility that Napoleon would have won the battle of Waterloo if he just had two tanks.

2. The plausibility or probability of a counterfactual has to be determined in its appropriate context, that is, in the context preceding the actual historical event. The historian must place him- or herself in the position of the contemporaries to whom the various possible alternatives were still available, for whom the selection was not closed by the actualization of one of them.

3. The possible alternatives have to be preserved in some sort of record: "We can only legitimately consider those hypothetical scenarios which contemporaries not only considered, but also committed to paper (or some other form of record) which has survived—and which has been identified as a valid source by historians" (1997, 83–87).

Ferguson's restrictions may be too stringent,[14] but at the moment they are the best we have for conducting counterfactual history as an integral part of historiography. The historians of Ferguson's group avoid counterfactual history of *longue durée* because it can be constructed only by unconstrained imagination. They focus on a relatively short span of historical time in which counterfactual alternatives are small in number, plausible, and even recorded.[15] A Fergusonian counterfactual historian recovers the "rejects" of decision makers (preserved in government records, planning papers, diplomatic exchanges, etc.) and revives actions that were considered but were prevented or failed.[16] Michael Burleigh's counterfactual study "Nazi Europe: What If Nazi Germany Had Defeated the Soviet Union?" is a telling example of the Fergusonian alternative history. Burleigh presents evidence drawn from German plans for the Germanization of Central and Eastern Europe and from experimental "ethnic cleansing" that was actually carried out in Poland. On the basis of this evidence he concludes: "We can thus see very clearly how a victorious Germany would have dealt with the territories of a dismembered Soviet Union (and, let us add, of Poland, Lithuania, Bohemia, and Moravia).

Plans survive in profusion. All we need to imagine to construct a credible counterfactual is a military victory" (1997, 326). Burleigh shows us very dramatically what would have happened in Europe sixty years ago if the sacrifice of millions had not prevented it.

Fictional representations of the past, we have claimed, cannot be a source of reliable historical knowledge. But Fergusonian counterfactuals are a special kind of fictional worlds constructed under specific constraints, constraints reflecting the epistemological principles of historical-knowledge acquisition and historical-worlds construction. A Fergusonian historian has to give up the unrestricted imagination of the fictionalist and submit his or hers to the requirements of evidence and testing, just as the "factual" historian does. Because Fergusonian counterfactual worlds are constructed in this way, they can make valuable contributions to historical knowledge. Reconstructing the paths not taken, the events prevented, the attempts failed, the counterfactual historians deepen our understanding of the past in expanding their historical worlds by domains of nonactualized but documented possibles. They contribute to the creation of a historiography based on the idea of possible worlds, a historiography of multidimensional models.

It should not escape our attention that the project of Fergusonian counterfactual history was formulated just at the time when the radical thinkers of the postmodern were denying the difference between history and fiction. Our study of the practice of counterfactual narratives allows us to add one more theoretical objection to the postmodern challenge to those formulated in the previous chapters. Even in the universe of counterfactual fictions a line can be drawn between those worlds that have no claim to historical validity, because they are inventions of free imagination, and those that are constructed by controlled imagination and legitimately pursue the cognitive efforts of historical research. A "minor" genre of writing about the past thus achieves a major theoretical significance: in the postmodern discussions of the relationship between fiction and history it reconfirms that the distinction between the *poietic* and the *noetic* reconstructions of the past is not abolished.

# NOTES

INTRODUCTION: *Remarks on Postmodernism*

1. Larry McCaffery, like Fokkema focusing on literary fiction, locates "the postmodern awakening" in the period 1960–75 (1986, xix).

2. Fokkema adds wealth to the conditions necessary for the emergence of postmodernism in a society: "Postmodernism . . . is linked to a particular way and view of life, common in the Western world and increasingly common in the affluent societies of East Asia and Latin America. . . . The Postmodernist preference for nonselection as a principle of text production coincides with an *embarras de choix* originating in favorable material conditions and seemingly unlimited technological potentialities" (1987, 234).

3. Dowe Fokkema considers McHale's use of the term *ontological* "misleading" because it "has the connotation of traditional philosophy, of serious and explicit reflection on ways of being, and very little of this can be found in postmodernist writing" (1997, 20–21). However, McHale obviously does not have in mind traditional philosophy's "reflection on ways of being." Rather, he takes the phrase *ontological problems* from the framework of possible worlds, where ontology means choices from numerous alternative possible worlds. Steven Connor, who explores the radical experimentation in postmodern culture, maintains that postmodern narratives are "inseparable from the nested proliferation of different worlds or orders of reality." He says that literary fiction took "the 'ontological' interest in creating and exploring other and multiple worlds" over from science fiction ([1989] 1997, 115, 134).

4. According to Hans Bertens, Hutcheon's theoretization marks an encounter between the postmodern and the postructuralist debates. It has been so influential that we can speak about "a Hutcheon school" (1997, 12).

5. In Russia, Julija Rajneke echoes this view. She constructs a "model" of postmodernism, suggesting as its main feature "play" *(igra)*: "Postmodernism plays with forms, signs, discourses, codes of various periods, styles, trends. The author plays with the text, with the readers. A playful attitude towards the word makes it possible to search for, and find, new senses hidden in it. . . . The postmodern-

ists love to play with virtual reality, use its means, they love to model rather than reflect reality" (2002, 36, 37).

6. There is no lack of critical arguments against the foundations and consequences of deconstruction by scholars young and old (see, e.g., Abrams 1977; Savan 1983; Rose 1984; Freundlieb 1988; Ellis 1989; and Pavel 1989). But Christopher Norris may be right when he claims that in "many passages" of his writings "Derrida says just the opposite" of what he originally claimed and that "his recent essays have laid increasing stress on this need to conserve what is specific to philosophy, namely its engagement with ethical, political and epistemological issues that cannot be reduced *tout court* to the level of an undifferentiated textual 'freeplay'" (1988, 12). Derrida's philosophy would thus neatly fit into Hutcheon's image of postmodernism—courting contradictions, loving paradoxes, but leaving them unresolved. But how do we argue with a self-contradictory philosophy? Anything can be derived from a contradiction.

7. As Thomas Pavel pointed out, the epistemology of deconstruction implies that "the debate is concluded and the file has been closed" (1989, 9). This was not the first time that rational inquiry into poetic art had been declared finished. Referring to German aesthetic idealism of the beginning of the nineteenth century, Boethius proclaimed without blushing: "The history of poetology is hereby brought to its end, even though it seems to continue an armchair existence in the theories of literary scholars harking back again and again to the claims of the Enlightenment" (1973, 133).

8. Catachresis is Miller's master figure, a manifestation of the very workings of meaning in language: "All words are initially catachreses. The distinction between literal and figurative is an alogical deduction or bifurcation from that primal misnaming" (1976, 29). Ironically, Miller thus arrives at a "unified totality" (Rimmon-Kenan 1980–81, 187), much grander than the structuralist totalization he had criticized.

9. Miller does exactly what all close analyses of poetic texts, including the structuralist poetics of the Prague school, have been doing: he describes the poetic text as an aesthetic phenomenon. The similarity between deconstructionist poetological praxis and Prague school poetics is not accidental; it has hidden roots in a common perception of what constitutes the basic features of poetic language. To my knowledge, this connection was first pointed out and documented by Peter Nesselroth in a paper presented, significantly, at the first post-Communist conference on the Czech structuralist Jan Mukařovský, in the spring of 1991. Specifically, Nesselroth linked Mukařovský's concept of de-automatization to the practice of deconstructive reading: "Deconstructive reading . . . depends on the systematic and perpetual de-automatization of all possible meanings in

words and expressions, whether they be spoken or written" (1999, 32; see also Doležel 2000).

10. Derek Attridge is more hesitant than Ulmer to differentiate applied grammatology of literary texts from deconstruction of philosophical writings. In a crucial passage, however, we read: "Derrida's writings on literary texts are . . . not commentaries in any conventional sense, not criticism, not interpretation. . . . They do not attempt to place, to master, or exhaust, or translate, or penetrate the literary work. Like all valuable readings of literature, they seek to make the text strange (or perhaps strangely familiar), offering not a reduced or simplified version of the text but one which operates at its own level of difficulty. . . . Each one is different in style, tone, manner, emphasis, argument, as it responds to a text that is different from all others. But it is not merely a matter of writing a poem in response to a poem; Derrida's texts on literature . . . remain fascinated by philosophical questions, and look for ways of letting the literary text's undoing of philosophy be heard" (1992, 16–17). After all, the very idea of Attridge's anthology is based on the assumption that there is a set of Derrida's writings on literature.

### CHAPTER ONE: *The Postmodern Challenge*

1. The English-speaking reader should be warned against Peter Wexler's unreliable translation (in Lane 1970). It is superseded by Stephen Bann's accurate and articulate rendering (in *Comparative Criticism,* 1981). In the following citations of Barthes's essay, my first reference is to the French original, and my second is to Bann's translation, although I take the liberty of modifying his wording when necessary based on a comparison with the original.

2. Before we leave the analytical part of Barthes's essay, we should note and keep for future reference one claim: discourses may be affirmative, negative, or interrogative. "Historical discourse," according to Barthes, is "uniformly assertive, affirmative": "we recount what has been, not what has not been, or what has been uncertain. . . . Historical discourse is not acquainted with negation (or only very rarely, in exceptional cases)" (71; 14). The postmodern Barthes allies himself with a very conservative view of history that denies legitimacy to any kind of conjecture or counterfactual speculation.

3. Reading carefully Barthes's quotation from Thierry, we notice that Thierry considers history a rhetorical exercise whose purpose is "de frapper et de convaincre tous les esprits" (75n13).

4. Parallel proposals to treat history as narrative were made by modern historians, especially W. B. Gallie in 1964. However, there is a substantial difference between these views of narrative history and those of the postmodernists. Louis

Mink summarizes Gallie's position as follows: "History does not as such [as narrative] differ from fiction, . . . insofar as it essentially depends on and develops our skill and subtlety in following stories. History does of course differ from fiction insofar as it is obligated to rest upon evidence of the occurrence in real space and time of what it describes and insofar as it must grow out of critical assessment of the received materials of history, including the analyses and interpretations of other historians" (1998, 124–25).

5. It is worth noting that White treats the terms *speculative philosophy of history* and *metahistory* as synonymous (Vann 1995, 65).

6. It has been almost forgotten that in *Metahistory* White considers, in addition to emplotment, two more traditional kinds of explanation of historical events, of assigning "meaning" to history (the quotation marks are his): by argument, logical explanation; and by ideology, ethical explanation. In later writings emplotment monopolized the stage.

7. The practitioners, not the theorist, should be blamed for the fact that the turmoil of human history is played out in only four archetypal plots. White remarks *en passant* that historians "tend to be naïve storytellers" (1973, 8n6). This is a strange admission given that according to the postmodern "poetics of history," narrating stories is the main ingredient of the historian's craft. One could equally blame the theorists for being rather poor narratologists: "No philosopher [of history] . . . produced any convincing criteria for deciding what constituted a narrative or how to recognize one" (Vann 1995, 51). While narratology has been established since the 1970s as the most active part of literary theory, among the theorists of history only Hayden White (1987) and Robert F. Berkhofer (1997) have taken notice, and they refer only to the mainstream of general narratology.

8. The project of *Metahistory* is, then, to show that "the 'historical realisms' of Michelet, Tocqueville and Ranke consisted of little more than critical elaborations of perspectives provided by [the] tropological strategies for processing experience in specifically 'poetic' ways. And in the 'realism' of Burkhardt one witnesses once more the fall into that Ironic condition from which 'realism' itself was supposed to liberate the historical consciousness of the age" (1973, 40).

9. The equation is supported by a push from the other side, by treating literary fiction as mimesis, as imitation or representation of reality: "The aim of the writer of a novel must be the same as that of the writer of a history. *Both wish to provide a verbal image of 'reality'*" (White 1978, 122, emphasis added). In this normative formulation, White not only takes recourse to an antiquated, certainly premodernist view of fiction but installs it as a general law of fiction making. It is worth noting that, as Ann Curthoys and John Docker point out, "an active opposition between history and literature is historically quite recent, a product of the

nineteenth century. In England and in Europe in the 'long eighteenth century' (1660–1830), history was viewed as a branch of literature" (2005, 50–51).

10. Natalie Zemon Davis arrives at the double equation by the same procedure of synonym substitution. In the introduction to her seductively titled book *Fiction in the Archives* she states: "Whenever I read these royal letters of pardon and remission . . . I marvel at the literary qualities of these texts, or, I might say, their 'fictional' qualities, by which I mean the extent to which their authors shape the events of a crime into a story. . . . I want to let the 'fictional' aspects of these documents be the center of analysis." She mitigates the damage by using the term *fiction* in its etymological rather than its common sense: "By 'fictional' I do not mean their [the documents'] feigned elements, but rather, using the other and broader sense of the root word *fingere,* their forming, shaping, and molding elements: the crafting of a narrative" (1987, 2–3). It should not escape our attention that Davis puts all the crucial words—*fictional, historical,* and *real*—in quotation marks. (The obsessive use of quotation marks around certain terms in postmodern writing deserves special study.) Davis aims at relativizing historiography at a deeper level: already the historian's cherished archival documents show features of fictionality. But we will be much less affected by this conclusion if we realize that Davis's documents are of a special kind—letters of remission, in which a convicted criminal, usually a murderer, asks the king for pardon. After all, such letters had to present a moving tale (as their professional writers knew all too well) in order to influence favorably the only person who could save a supplicant's life.

11. According to Mark Poster, "Hayden White was isolated and virtually excluded from the profession with the publication of *Metahistory* in 1973" (1997, 154). Even in 1991, according to Richard Vann, "only about one per cent of members of the American Historical Association listed 'philosophy of history and historiography' as either a primary or secondary field of scholarly interest. Although there are many fewer American philosophers than historians, about seven times as many philosophers identified themselves as interested in the philosophy of history" (Ankersmit and Kellner 1995, eds., 252n95). Although citation statistics are no more than symptoms of "popularity," Vann's numbers are interesting: "There are well over a thousand citations of White's work in philosophy of history in . . . twenty years. That averages over fifty a year; but the series starts very small (only one in 1974, and still only eighteen in 1978) and rises to close to a hundred per year in the late 1980s and early 1990s" (1998, 146).

12. These modes of emplotment might, however, be admitted if they "had been set forth in a pointedly ironic way," as in Art Spiegelman's comic book *Maus,* which represents the Holocaust "in a mode of bitter satire, with Germans por-

trayed as cats, Jews as mice, and Poles as pigs." We might question the tastefulness of such a representation, but we have to agree with White that it is not "conventional history" (1992, 40, 41). Spiegelman's comics are not "historical narrative" and therefore have no bearing on White's argument. A 1997 film about a German concentration camp in Italy, *La vita è bella* (released in the United States under the title *Life is Beautiful*), was promoted as a comedy. In fact, it is a tragic story that ends with the hero's death.

13. Berel Lang remains most forceful in his rebuttal of the postmodern challenge. He points out that the postmodern theorists fail "to consider—let alone to defend—the implications of their own views of historical representation," that they do not mention "the costs," "the price of their own proposal." The Holocaust is a test of historical representation not because of its uniqueness as a historical event "but because the consequences that hinge on the status of alternate Holocaust narratives [i.e., narratives of denial] . . . demonstrate graphically what is at stake in the issue of historical representation more generally" (1997, 431; see also 1998, 249).

14. Jenkins's 1997 volume is very useful; in part 2 opposing arguments from three prominent journals of the profession, from Friedlander's 1992 proceedings, and from the "symposium" on the Holocaust published in *History and Theory* 1994 and 1995 are reprinted side by side.

15. It is quite surprising that the postmodern narrativists have not considered theoretically this kind of historiography. As I mentioned in chapter I, Barthes shook the nuisance off with a casual, ad hoc remark.

16. Perhaps late postmodernism has become extremely radical because it feels threatened in its dominion. There are strong indications of a new trend at the beginning of the new millennium that criticizes and in many respects reverses the "linguistic turn." "It should be clear by now," writes Gabrielle Spiegel, that "the new master concepts in post-linguistic turn historiography are experience and practice" (2005, 18). Her anthology (Spiegel, ed., 2005) brings together an impressive array of post-postmodern theories of history. Allan Megill's latest work (2007) is also symptomatic of the changed atmosphere in the discussion of the philosophy of history. His book is no longer concerned with the refutation of arguments coming from the history of the "linguistic turn." In fact, when he identifies the "current fashion," he sees it in (mostly popularizing) publications that "evangelize" and offer an "immediate" experience of the past. "The advertising [for these books] uniformly suggests that the consumers of these histories will be brought into direct contact with the action" (211). In other words, for Megill the challenge to history comes not from subtle, abstract theories of language but from rough, intensive pressures of the consumer culture. This "contemporary guide" propagates a return to the traditional problems and previously suggested

solutions of the epistemology of historiography. I do not believe, however, that contemporary historians can simply skip over the postmodern challenge and return to traditional ways of making history. To dismiss the postmodern critique and practice as "dangerous" or "hype" is, in fact, an attempt to restore the quiet days of undisturbed, unexamined epistemological principles.

CHAPTER TWO: *Representation of the Past and Possible Worlds*

1. The most important document proving the cross-disciplinary scope of the notion of possible worlds is Allén 1989. Recently Marie-Laure Ryan explored the two limits of the outreach of possible worlds, cosmology (with quantum mechanics) and narratology (Ryan 2006).

2. I have in mind performatives uttered by actual people in the actual world, that is, in the world governed by laws of nature as we know them. In this world magic performatives are infelicitous (to use Austin's apposite term) because they contradict its "order." Magic performatives are, however, possible in belief worlds, that is, in the worlds of individuals and groups who believe that by uttering an appropriate, usually ritual formula they can bring about events that violate the laws of nature. They might even believe that these performatives can change the states of the actual world by performing "miracles." Magic performatives and miracles are thus always relative to belief worlds, which admit the supernatural (the physically impossible) but are not effective in the actual world, which is natural and therefore admits only physically possible states and events.

3. What follows in this section is a revised discussion of the concept of possible worlds found in Doležel 1998, 12–15.

4. There is even an existential import to possible worlds, stated succinctly by Janet H. Murray: "To be alive in the 20th century is to be aware of the alternative possible selves, of alternative possible worlds, and of the limitless interacting stories of the actual world" (1997, x). The proceedings of Nobel Symposium 55 testify to the reach of possible-world semantics, but as already mentioned in the preface, general history was not discussed at the symposium.

5. Using a different term, Richard Kirkham proposes the same definition: "Of particular interest is the subset of *naturally* possible worlds, which is the subset of worlds having all and only the same laws of nature as the actual world" (1992, 15).

6. David Lewis, emphasizing that "things in different worlds are *never* identical," links the various incarnations of one thing in different worlds by the "counterpart relation," which is "a relation of similarity"; thus, he seems to assume that the counterparts (have to) share some essential properties. But his relationship of similarity is flexible enough to link the Hitler of history and a Hitler who led

"a blameless life." In the end, Lewis disarms all those who might classify him as essentialist with a charming innocence: "The essences of things are settled only to the extent that the counterpart relation is, and the counterpart relation is not very settled at all" (1983, 27–29, 42).

7. Roderick Chisholm considers the term *actual* ambiguous and proposes instead "the world that obtains" or "the prevailing world" (1981, 129). This might be a useful terminological suggestion, but it only confirms the need to assign to one possible world exclusive ontological status.

8. This tactic is not entirely novel. R. G. Collingwood, trying to define the difference between fiction and history, resorted to the opposition between a multitude of worlds of fiction and one, and only one, world of history: "Purely imaginary worlds cannot clash and need not agree; each is a world unto itself. But there is only one historical world, and everything in it must stand in some relation to everything else, even if that relation is only topographical and chronological" (1993, 246). W. B. Gallie perceived the difficulties of this position (1964, 57–62) but did not offer a possible-worlds alternative.

9. Herein the term *model* is used as a cognitive tool applicable not only to historical universals ("laws" of a society or epoch) but also, and primarily, to ordered sets of particular units—sequences of historical events, constellations of historical persons, designs of individual periods, and so on.

10. Georg Iggers adds an interesting comment to Braudel's suggestions: "Michel Foucault considers the idea of *one* history to be an invention of modern times, which have already ended. Most *Annales* historians would concur. In the place of one historical time, they see a plurality of coexisting times, not only among different civilizations but also within each civilization. This idea is most clearly developed in the structure of Braudel's Mediterranean book, which distinguishes three different times, each with its own speed: the almost stationary time of the Mediterranean as a geographical space *(long durée)*, the slow time of changes in social and economic structures *(conjonctures)*, and the fast time of political events *(événements)*" (1997, 56–57).

11. The so-called syndrome "consists of a diverse set of symptoms whereby the trauma of the Occupation, and particularly that trauma of the internal divisions within France reveals itself in political, social, and cultural life" (Rousso 1995, 647).

12. How to test the adequacy of historical models and of models in general is a complex epistemological problem that is beyond the scope of this book. Let me just mention that certain notions from the traditional testing of historical representations could be usefully appropriated, such as the notion of "agreed-upon facts." According to Raymond Martin, at any given time historians "always accept a large body of agreed-upon facts. . . . Over time the status of many of these

putative facts may change from agreed-upon to highly questionable. However, . . . changes in the status of agreed-upon facts are slow and piecemeal. It is never the case that most such 'facts' change from agreed-upon to highly questionable at the same time" (1998, 398–99). Even Hans Kellner, who is no friend of "facts," grudgingly recognizes the supraindividuality of the cognitive activity of reconstructing the past: "Let us suppose that the profession of history in a non-totalitarian world functions more or less as it represents itself. It certifies the skills and standards of its members through granting degrees; it informally designates the hierarchy of prestige and reputations that determines professional credibility; it culls published material for errors of documentation or false inferences. It is able to maintain its control of justified belief; what the consensus of professional historians believe to be the best information and judgment is taken to be the best information and judgement. Most importantly, this process is dynamic; the work of criticism is ongoing. This is how the system is supposed to work, and I believe, that it does, for the most part" (1997, 407–8).

13. For a study of fantastic worlds in the period of realism, see Traill 1996; the world of the "modern myth" is reconstructed in Doležel 1998, 185–98.

14. This statement is not true of all historical periods and of all cultures, but it is correct with regard to relatively recent occidental history (perhaps since Voltaire). Representations of the past that included supernatural worlds were common in some past periods of our culture and still are in some other cultures, but today they appear to us as mythological, not historical, worlds. In contemporary occidental culture secularity is a defining feature of historical representation.

15. Elena Semino (1997, 115) gives an example of a nursery rhyme that "raises an interesting ambiguity as to the kind of world it projects: 'Yesterday upon the stair / I met a man who wasn't there. / He wasn't there again today. / I wish that man would go away!' Consider the implications of taking the expression 'who wasn't there' literally. . . . You may also have become aware of a different reading of the rhyme, which results from relating the expression 'wasn't there' to the idiom 'not to be all there,' which means 'to be simple' or 'to be silly in the head.'" The second interpretation changes an impossible world into a possible one.

16. Even in the domain of fiction the construction of impossible worlds is achieved only at the price of ruining the entire enterprise of fiction making (see Doležel 1998, 165).

17. With respect to fictional counterparts of actual places, the principle of verisimilitude has been rejected by Ruth Ronen: "a) It is impossible to demarcate essential properties of Paris which do (or should) recur in each of its literary constructions; b) diverse descriptive sets can be attributed to the same name in different fictional worlds and therefore descriptions that replace a name in one particular fictional world cannot be transferred or applied to other pos-

sible worlds" (1994, 503). Discussing the opposition of biography and fiction, Dorrit Cohn emphasizes "the biographer's constraint and the novelist's freedom" (1989, 6).

18. Tolstoy thus was able to present the campaign of 1812 as a war in which all classes of Russian society fought enthusiastically. He created a radical contrast between Napoleon, who "wants to control history, who is convinced that he controls history," and Kutuzov, who believes only in the force of the people. He employed the subtle narrative device of "making strange" to strengthen the contrast between the French and the Russian story line. Shklovsky concludes that *War and Peace* "is not history" but "canonization of a legend" ([1928] 1970, 64, 72, 60, 71, 75).

19. Let me emphasize that fictional semantics has to differentiate between gaps and implicit fictional facts; the former are irrecoverable, the latter are recovered by inference (for details see Doležel 1995 and 1998, 169–77).

20. "Confronted with the great diversity of nonrepetitive individual or mass happenings, the historian must choose which 'facts' he considers important and which he must discard as 'irrelevant'" (Baron 1986, 15).

21. Trevor-Roper states the bond between discovering sources and writing history: "When I found myself in possession of these . . . major sources, I believed that I was in a position to reconstruct and perhaps explain the life of Backhouse" (1976, 9).

22. Frege does not use the term *fiction*, but his German *Dichtung* is as close as one could get to the English term.

23. A theory of authentication is presented in Doležel 1998, 145–68.

24. To distinguish the sentences of the fictional text from those about the fictional world, Pavel designated the latter as ersatz sentences (1975/76). John Hayden Woods dramatized the truth functionality of ersatz sentences by calling them "bet sensitive": one could win a bet on "Sherlock Holmes lived on Baker Street" but lose a bet on "Sherlock Holmes lived on Berczy Street" (1974, 13–14).

## CHAPTER THREE: *Postmodern Historical Worlds: Simon Schama*

1. All this does not mean that the "new" domains of history were totally unknown to historians of previous eras. Marnie Hughes-Warrington, for example, noting the appreciation expressed by prominent members of the Annales school, writes: "They acknowledged their debt to Michelet for helping them to see the importance of describing the past in its totality, recognizing the relationship between geography and history, drawing on a wide range of sources and looking for the details of life among ordinary people" (2000, 230).

2. The new branches, especially microhistory, the history of everyday life, and gender history, sprouted largely in response to political stimuli (see Noiriel 1998, 110–11, 114–15, 122–23); they quickly joined the old branches of history as legitimate subfields.

3. In saying "again" I am alluding to Trevor-Roper's restatement (1969, 23–24) of Carlyle's observation that Scott's historical novels taught the writers of history that "the bygone ages of the world were actually filled by living men, not by protocols, state-papers, controversies, and abstractions of men." For Ranke, according to Ann Curthoys and John Docker (2005, 61–62), "Scott was important for inspiring a nineteenth-century interest in history, and his novels were, Ranke admits, 'attraction enough for me, and I read these works with lively interest.' But he also 'took objection to them.' He found himself 'offended' by the way that Scott had knowingly created historical portraits that 'seemed, even in particular details, to be completely contradictory to the historical evidence.'"

4. In a similar spirit Peter Burke calls for a synthesis of the numerous contemporary branches of history, especially of the two old rivals—the history of events and the history of structures (1992a, 236–37; 1992b, 18–21).

5. Rosenstone refers to White's essay "The Burden of History," in which the "metahistorian" complains that historians wholly "eschew the techniques of literary representation which Joyce, Yeats, and Ibsen have contributed to modern culture. There have been no significant attempts at surrealistic, expressionistic, or existentialist historiography" (qtd. in Rosenstone 2004, 4). Too bad. It would be extremely interesting to read, say, a surrealistic history.

6. Rosenstone provides an impressive list of modern fictional-narrative techniques and devices: "the present tense; the self-reflexive, narration in the second person (direct address to the reader and, sometimes, to the historical characters); narration in the first person (not of the author but of his subjects); a character named 'the biographer,' who occasionally enters the pages . . . ; and, finally, an occasional shift of time and space within a single sentence, a flash back or forwards or sideways" (2004, 3–4).

7. The essays in this volume were originally published in the journal *Rethinking History: The Journal of Theory and Practice,* launched by Munslow and Rosenstone in 1997.

8. For the concept of universalist mimesis, see Doležel 1998, 7–8.

9. Referring to another prominent work by Schama, *The Embarrassment of Riches: An Interpretation of Dutch Culture in the Golden Age* (1987), Ivan Gaskell praises him not only for a "sophisticated use of visual material" but also for pressing "a vast range of material into service, including poetry, choreography, travellers' accounts, notarial documents, court records, prints and paintings" (1992,

188, 189). The combination of meticulous research, careful documentation, and vivid presentation is also evident in Schama's art-historical work, especially in *Rembrandt's Eyes* (1999).

10. Schama sees the obvious danger: having followed the precedent of nineteenth-century narrative history, his work "runs the risk of being seen as a mischievously old-fashioned piece of storytelling" (1989, xvi). Schama will avoid this risk by a radical transformation of narrative history.

11. Steven G. Crowell calls Carr's position "narrative realism," in contrast to the "narrative idealism" of Ankersmit and other postmodern "metahistorians" (1998, 238–42). Carr's argument in favor of narrative as a constituent of "real life" is very close to Barbara Hardy's earlier (1968) conception: "Narrative, like lyric or dance, is not to be regarded as an aesthetic invention used by artists to control, manipulate and order experience, but as a primary act of mind transferred to art from life. . . . For we dream in narrative, daydream in narrative, remember, anticipate, hope, despair, believe, doubt, plan, revise, criticize, construct, gossip, learn, hate and love by narrative" (qtd. in Mink 1998, 135). It has to be noted that Mink disagrees with this position: "It seems truer to say that narrative qualities are transferred from art to life. We could learn to tell stories of our lives from nursery rhymes, or from culture-myths, if we had any, but it is from history and fiction that we learn how to tell and to understand *complex* stories, and how it is that stories answer questions" (135).

12. In a different context, Schama returns to the problem of history and fiction: "This is not to say, I should emphasize, that I scorn the boundary between fact and fiction. It is merely to imply that even in the most austere scholarly report from the archives, the inventive faculty—selecting, pruning, editing, commenting, interpreting, delivering judgments—is in full play. This is not a naively relativist position that insists that the lived past is *nothing* more than an artificially designed text." He adds a somewhat surprising comment: "Despite the criticism of dug-in positivists, I know of no thoughtful commentator on historical narrative who seriously advances this view" (1991, 322).

13. The affair is discussed in Schama 1989, ch. 6; the documentation appears on pp. 888–89.

14. Schama developed the craft of shaping the historical world of revolutionary change in his first major work, *Patriots and Liberators: Revolution in the Netherlands, 1780–1813* (1977). The historical world of *Patriots and Liberators* prefigures that of *Citizens*. Although Schama recognizes the indigenous features of the Dutch revolutions, he emphasizes their strong similarities to the revolution in France. The semantic structure of Schama's historical worlds brings forth the homology of the three revolutionary events (two Dutch revolutions and one French).

15. For a discussion of "the science of the individual," see Doležel 2000.

16. Schama makes a useful distinction between "regulated" crowd activities (such as religious processions), spontaneous crowd fellowships (such as spectators at "ballooning" events), and instinctive acting of the mob, *"un attroupement"* (1989, 131).

17. Overall, Schama tells us, "the French Revolution was obsessed with the model of the Roman Republic" (1989, 169).

18. Does Schama in the end support the traditional hypothesis that the prime factor leading to the outbreak of the revolution was the fiscal crisis of the French crown and a general social crisis in French society? Schama smartly complicates this question by distinguishing between the fall of the monarchy and the revolution. "If the causes of the French Revolution are complex, the causes of the downfall of the monarchy are not. The two phenomena are not identical, since the end of absolutism in France did not of itself entail a revolution of such transformative power as actually came to pass in France. But the end of the old regime was the necessary condition of the beginning of a new, and that was brought about, in the first instance, by a cash-flow crisis. It was the politicization of the money crisis that dictated the calling of the Estates-General" (1989, 62). One is left wondering whether there was not one major weakness in the explanatory nexus of the master of narrative history: the fact that in social processes the assignment of agents and the determination of the chain of event causality are much more complex than in private actions and perhaps substantially different.

19. "Let us be terrible so that the people will not have to be," Danton declared (1989, 707). In vain, Pierre Vergniaud, the star orator of the Girondins, warned his compatriots: "So, citizens, it must be feared that the Revolution, like Saturn, successively devouring its children, will engender, finally, only despotism with the calamities that accompany it" (714).

20. Jacques Revel enumerates the following social entities acting in historical worlds: "a community (village, parish, city, district, and so on), an occupational group, an order, a class" (1995, 498). I assume that armies are included under occupational groups.

21. While environmental history and cultural geography are claimed to be "new" branches of historiography, it should be remembered that attention to environmental factors in general, and to locales in particular, has been a feature of historiography since antiquity (Barnes 1962, 349–55). The issue is clarified by Brian Fay in his introduction to a special issue of *History and Theory* devoted to environmental history. Fay writes: "Historians have always known that the natural environment plays a significant role in how humans behave, relate to one another, and organize themselves. . . . But . . . only in the past twenty-five years or so have historians methodically pursued a systematic exploration of this inter-

change, in the process establishing a distinct branch of history: environmental history" (2003, 1).

22. Burke mentions two historical works in which the past is written "backwards": B. D. Sumner's *Survey of Russian History* (1944), which is organized by topics; and Norman Davies's history of Poland, *Heart of Europe* (1984), "a narrative which focuses on what the author calls 'the past in Poland's present'" (1992a, 244).

23. A literary intertext—Rudyard Kipling's *Puck of Pook's Hill,* with its fantastic story of time travel—and childhood memories of the river Thames ("to go upstream was . . . to go backward" [1989, 5]) were the initial inspirations for Schama's method.

24. Making explicit Schama's implicit link, we should point to the American nineteenth-century historian Francis Parkman as an inspiring influence. His *France and England in North America* (1892), Schama wrote previously, is "an American history which would have the forest as its principal character." Schama shares with Parkman the wish "to give lyric expression to his exhilaration with the landscape and history" (1991, 48, 50).

25. In his meticulous survey of research in environmental history J. R. McNeill detects some encouraging developments counteracting the deplored environmental destruction, the "declensionist tendency" (2003, 35–36).

26. This plot pattern is known in historiography. A pure example of it is Edward Gibbon's ([1909] 1974) chapter 44 (in volume 4), devoted to the evolution of Roman jurisprudence. Starting with a presentation of the legal codices of Justinian, Gibbon descends to the beginnings of Roman law at the time of the founders and first kings of the city and then proceeds forward in time to the "immortal works" of Justinian.

27. "The obedient walker was required to proceed from fountain to fountain, from watery births (such as Venus's) to watery deaths (such as Adonis's) in a particular order, sometimes moving from a wild to a 'civilized' classical setting, sometimes the reverse" (1996, 275).

28. Schama, misled by an obsolete French work on Bedřich Smetana, maintains that the river flows from the Tatra Mountains (1996, 363).

29. Schama does not miss, although mentioning only *en passant,* the "new" representation of the (mountain) landscape—the map. Maps join landscape paintings in his historical world.

30. It is regrettable that Schama overlooked Roland Barthes's "excavation" of myth in modern culture (see Barthes 1957).

31. Wilhelm Heinrich Riehl was a German sociologist of "field and forest" who in his three-volume work *The Natural History of the German People* (1851–

55) promoted the idea of *Heimat* as "a physical topography with specific customs and idioms" (Schama 1996, 113).

32. The following is an example of Schama's meticulous revelation of the aesthetic and ideological features of paintings: "While St. George is set parallel to the plane of the forest, as if in consort with it, the hapless *chasseur* faces it dead-on, pulled into its interior by the relentlessly commanding path leading nowhere good. For where, in the Altdorfer, the vegetation is pierced by light, exposing a space beyond, in the Friedrich there is only blackness. Like Varus's centurions, the *chasseur* is surrounded and dwarfed by the impenetrable line of evergreens, the massed troops of the reborn Germania" (1996, 106).

33. The tradition can be attested by numerous references to Gibbon's text. Two examples should suffice: "I am not insensible to the benefits of elegant luxury; yet I reflect with some pain that, if the importers of silk had introduced the art of printing, practiced by the Chinese, the comedies of Menander and the entire decades of Livy would have been perpetuated in the editions of the sixth century"; and "I desire to believe, but I dare not affirm, that Belissarius sincerely rejoiced in the triumph of Narses" ([1909] 1974, 4:250, 454).

34. For an explanation of the concept of metafiction, see Doležel 1998, 162.

35. It is difficult to comprehend why Schama's assertion of the fictional character of *Dead Certainties* is ignored by commentators and critics. Dorrit Cohn states that although Schama's afterword to *Dead Certainties* "designates the two pieces it contains as 'historical novellas,' his critics severely objected to his use of such techniques as interior monologue to present the thoughts of real persons. Gordon S. Wood, for one, found this book highly confusing on this score, reproaching Schama for wanting to 'have it both ways' and leaving it unclear 'just what his experiment in narration is trying to accomplish'" (1999, 157). Berkhofer claims that the book "is presented as an experiment in historical narration" (1997, 280); see also above, sec. 3.1.

36. Perhaps historical fiction arose in the ancient, "Herodotian" tradition of the reconstruction of the past. In Schama's presentation, Herodotus, in contrast to Thucydides ("an early paragon of objectivity, of critical use of sources, of dispassionate analytical investigation") recommends himself by "his relish for gossip, his intuitive understanding of the idiosyncrasies of climate and geography, his primitive ethnography, his unabashed subjectivities, the winning mishmash of hearsay and record, real and fantastic" (Schama 1991, 325).

37. In a typically fictional move, Schama takes advantage of the uncertainties regarding the persons who attended Wolfe in his last hour "to use first-hand accounts of the action in the construction of my own witness" (1991, 329).

38. It is interesting that in a "prosaic" and "feeble" rendition of the scene ex-

ecuted by the painter Edward Penny in 1763, the General is attended by only two officers (1991, 29–30).

39. Court proceedings have attracted historians for yet another reason: even some proceedings from the remote past are relatively well documented. Schama's fictionalized history of Professor Webster's trial joins two major works of postmodern microhistory based on court documents—Natalie Zemon Davis's *Return of Martin Guerre* (1983) and Carlo Ginzburg's *The Cheese and the Worms* (1992). A much later trial is reconstructed in Berenson's microhistory (1992; see also above, sec. 3.1).

40. In preceding sections, quotations from Longfellow and Milton are inserted.

41. For a general discussion of this kind of "digressions," see Doležel 1998, 27.

CHAPTER FOUR: *Postmodern Historical Fiction*

1. Cohn comes to terms with the term *historical novel* by taking it "quite literally: its noun indicates (to use Döblin's words) that it 'is, in the first place, a novel'; its adjective points to the fact that, although 'it isn't history,' the historical dimension is (may be considered to be) more importantly involved in certain novels than in others. What is more, conceiving the genre in this broad and elastic way ties the works one assigns to it more solidly to the fiction side of the great divide—the divide I have been highlighting throughout this volume" (1999, 162), that is, the divide between fiction and history.

2. A more recent, very meticulous study of the genesis of *War and Peace* is Feuer 1996.

3. "Historical novels and films which blend fact and fancy are often enjoyable and sell well. However, one cannot respect them as sources of reliable information about the past" (McCullagh 1998, 308).

4. According to Elisabeth Wesseling (1991, 2), in North American literature "the core of this corpus [of postmodern historical fiction] comprises such novels as John Barth's *The Sot-Weed Factor* (1960), Thomas Pynchon's *V.* (1963) and *Gravity's Rainbow* (1973), Thomas Berger's *Little Big Man* (1964), Kurt Vonnegut's *Slaughterhouse-Five or The Children's Crusade* (1969), Ishmael Reed's *Mumbo Jumbo* (1972), R. L. Doctorow's *Ragtime* (1974) and Robert Coover's *The Public Burning* (1977)." Tim Gauthier remarks that "to possess and renarrate the past" is "an obsession in contemporary British writing" (2006, 177). (Fokkema's list of fictional texts published in North America in the 1960s and 1970s that in his view "and that of many other critics were predominantly read and appreciated as specimens of postmodernism" [1997, 27] does not include Doctorow's *Ragtime.*)

5. Umberto Eco, who as a fictionalist contributed to the development of the postmodern historical novel, takes these norms to be generally characteristic of historical fiction: "One of the basic fictional agreements of every historical novel is that however many imaginary characters are introduced in the story, everything else has to more or less correspond to what happened in that era in the real world" (1994, 107).

6. Wesseling adds: "We do not find any major infringements upon accepted chronology in modernist texts, contrary to postmodernist novels, which may shock the reader with blatant anachronisms such as a *fin-de-siècle* Vienna which is besieged by the Turks, or a Moses who gives a rock concert. These offenses against 'canonized history' . . . may be regarded as the most controversial, as well as least understood, feature of postmodernist writing" (1991, 93).

7. The first pair appears in Guy Davenport's "Aeroplanes at Brescia," the second in Pynchon's *Gravity's Rainbow,* the third in Robert Coover's *Public Burning.* We should add the fictional meeting between Morgan and Ford in Doctorow's *Ragtime.*

8. It should be noted, however, that even Bradbury cannot avoid the truth-functional concepts of "fact," "error," "flaw," and so on. As far as conspiracy theories of history are concerned, "to call into question the reliability of official history" is certainly quite different from implying that "history itself may be a form of fiction." "Historians of the world's secret history" do not erase the boundary between history and fiction; rather, they replace a historical world with a fictional one.

9. It helps that "these novelists often demonstrate at least a working knowledge of postmodern and poststructuralist theory, which then exercises a direct influence on the kind of fiction they produce. Writers like Martin Amis, Peter Ackroyd and Rushdie import criticism and theory directly into their novels, while others, like Byatt and David Lodge, situate their fictions literally in academic settings" (Gauthier 2006, 5–6).

10. It is too bad that in the end Thiher succumbs to the standard interpretation of this issue: "Our fictions continue to bear witness to the presence of the absence signified even as they decry its absence" (1990, 31).

11. This statement is meant to put to rest the often emphasized interpolation of Heinrich von Kleist's novella *Michael Kohlhaas* (1810) into *Ragtime,* particularly the taking of Kleist's hero as the prototype of Coalhouse Walker. (For a survey of critical opinions on this issue, see Williams 1996, 29–32.) Doctorow himself acknowledged this intertextual connection but proclaimed it to be his homage to the German Romantic. There is no more than a superficial resemblance between Kleist's sixteenth-century German hero and Doctorow's twentieth-century black American hero.

12. Almost every critic dealing with *Ragtime* asks what is historical fact and what is fiction. In the framework of fictional worlds this question is of minor importance, or rather it is transformed into the question, which fictional persons have, and which do not have, prototypes in the actual past? On this question I agree with Barbara Foley, who wrote that Doctorow "treats his major characters and major actions as fictive constructs. As in more traditional historical novels, data drawn from presumably extratextual sources enter the text primarily to corroborate the text's thematic design and are incorporated into a fictive totality" (1986, 14). McHale has emphasized that including prominent historical persons in a fictional world is not a privilege of postmodern historical fiction. But his meticulous listings suggest that crowding the fictional world with such persons and creating bizarre constellations is a favorite postmodern device (see McHale 1987, 84–86, 243nn2, 3; see also III.2 in the present work).

13. Jacob Riis's colored map of Manhattan is a perfect representation of this mosaic: "Riis made color maps of Manhattan's ethnic population. Dull gray for Jews—their favorite color, he said. Blue for the thrifty German. Black for the African. Green for the Irishman. And yellow for the cat-clean Chinaman. . . . Add dashes of color for Finns, Arabs, Greeks, and so on, and you have a crazy quilt, Riis cried, a crazy quilt of humanity!" (Doctorow 1974, 15–16).

14. McHale, who calls *Ragtime* "a late-modernist historical fiction," admits nevertheless that it violates "classical constraints," notably "in the fictional Coalhouse Walker's occupation of the Morgan Library" (1987, 88).

15. Carol Harter and James R. Thompson seemingly saved mimesis by practicing without restraint universalist mimetic interpretation (for the term see Doležel 1998, 8–9): "J. P. Morgan is an idea, the creative drive of capitalism atrophied into selfish and absurd eccentricity; Henry Ford is one of Faulkner's Snopes clan come north, the ruthless force of a single mechanical idea; Emma Goldman is the embodiment of sexual and political idealism; Harry Houdini represents the dilemma of the modern artist. . . . Father portrays the privilege and ineffectuality of the WASP; Coalhouse Walker embodies the natural aristocracy of the black; Tateh dramatizes the creative energy of the immigrant" (1990, 59–60).

16. One critical comment in support of my position comes from Harter and Thompson, which state that Doctorow rejected "an overarching linear plot line in favor of cleverly collated stories of his three generic families and the historical figures with whom they often interact. Cinematically constructed out of a series of scenes, situations, and interwoven stories, the plot is protean and constantly shifting, denying the reader the comfort of any continuous line of development, although it generally moves ahead in time. Nor do the public events provide a clear cause and effect continuity. Though it starts in 1902 and concludes with World War I, the effect is not one of historical chronicle but rather of context—a

sort of collage of people and events located roughly in the ragtime era" (1990, 55).

17. Christopher D. Morris speaks about and documents "many empty coincidences in the novel" (2002, 101).

18. Corinne Saunders assigns to "romance moments" a "powerful appeal" precisely because "they convey fundamental human emotions: they are transhistorical" (2004, 1).

19. Most critics of *Possession* write about the novel as a blend of the traditional and the postmodern. According to Jackie Buxton, "the novel offers modernist ideology in postmodernist guise" (2001, 103). Campbell observes that the novel combines "realist and experimental techniques" (2004, 118). These observations confirm my general characterization of the novel as "moderate postmodernism." And we might recall here McHale, with his "crossovers" from modernist to postmodernist writing (1987, 3–25).

20. Katharina Rennhak goes so far in her metafictional zeal as to reconstruct (the purely fictional poet) Randolph Ash's view of historiography: "A good historian is . . . always also a poet" (2002, 168). She does, however, differentiate Ash's view from that of Hayden White.

21. The historians' story exhibits typical features of the epistemic quest. Devices advancing the quest—coincidence (Michell and Bailey's meeting Lady Bailey by chance) and good luck (Michell and Bailey's discovery of the Ash-LaMotte correspondence under LaMotte's dolls)—alternate with devices that hamper it—retardation (Sir George's refusal to release the correspondence only after he takes "advice") (Byatt 1990, 90).

22. Only a stubbornly naïve mimetic interpreter would start looking for the prototypes of Ash, LaMotte, and other fictional persons of the past. And what would such an interpreter find? Just banal general similarities.

23. One could argue that *Possession* is not a historical novel, because the past here is a fictional construct. Counterparts of historical persons are very marginal and play no role in the story. But we have to take into account that Byatt's construct of the past is so authentic that it is a perfect substitute for the actual Victorian English literature. The epistemic quest for this past reinforces its authenticity. Thanks to this feature, *Possession* satisfies the dyadic-world requirement of our definition of historical fiction, while at the same time representing its "deviant" postmodern variety.

24. Textual collage is certainly one of the prime features of postmodern literature (and beyond). It originates in the modernist collage but is radicalized both in the breadth and in the weakening of structural and functional restrictions. It indicates, perhaps, that in many respects postmodernism is radical modernism.

CHAPTER FIVE: *Counterfactual Narratives of the Past*

1. Social scientists influenced by systems or games theory are critical of the *ceteris paribus* reconstructions. Thus Lars-Erik Cederman, discussing John Mueller's argument of the "irrelevance of nuclear weapons," writes: "The problem with Mueller's account is that he explicitly traces postwar history as it actually happened (including the Cuban missile crisis!) while merely 'subtracting' nuclear technology. This is a clear example of superficially rewritten history . . . because it is unlikely that crises that actually occurred in the nuclear postwar world would actually have taken place in the non-nuclear case, a point that becomes particularly acute with respect to the Cuban missile crisis. How could one envisage such a crisis in the absence of nuclear missiles? It is hard to avoid the conclusion that in these cases a more holistic approach is needed. Rather than attempting to break the independent variables out of their context while holding everything else equal, it is necessary to take more than one step back and to consider entire 'possible worlds'" (1996, 253).

2. Gavriel Rosenfeld altogether ignores this distinction when he points out that "during the last decade, the genre of counterfactual speculation known as 'alternative history' has emerged seemingly out of nowhere to become one of the most fertile fields of historical enquiry." He might be exaggerating here; after all, most historians are still skeptical or outright hostile to this kind of enquiry. But he is certainly right when he states that "these narratives have appeared in a multiplicity of forms, novels, short stories, films, television programs, comic books, historical monographs and essays, and internet web sites. . . . Alternative history has become a veritable phenomenon in contemporary Western culture" (2002, 90, 91).

3. McKnight points to the novel *Napoléon et la conquête du monde* (1836), by Louis-Napoléon Geoffroy-Chateau, as the first representative work of the genre (1994, 13–15). For a more recent contribution to the history of counterfactual historical fiction, especially in the Romance languages, see Rodiek 1997. However, Rodiek does not raise any theoretical questions and incorrectly claims that Ferguson "took up the tradition of the Squire volume" (127n23; see also below, sec. 4).

4. Abendsen's novel provides an intertextual link between the main participants of Dick's story. In this function it is joined by the Chinese book of oracles, *I Ching*. In a technologically highly developed civilization almost everybody consults the oracle before making any significant decision. McKnight points out the metafictional relationship between Dick's and Abendsen's novels: "*The Grasshopper Lies Heavy* is a window through which the reader's world appears, but it

is also a mirror in which *The Man in the High Castle* and the reader's relationship to it are reflected" (1994, 103).

5. A "Note" at the end of Harris's book provides relevant details of the factual fate of the historical counterparts.

6. Johannes Bulhof suggests that "determinism is irrelevant to most uses of modal and counterfactual claims" (1999, 159).

7. The Custodian, a youthful Archangel, describes the Archives as the embodiment of the idea of counterfactual history, very much in the spirit of Trevor-Roper and von Wright (and Jorge Luis Borges): "At each and every instant of Time, however brief you suppose it, the line of events forks like the stem of a tree putting forth twin branches. . . . One of these branches represents the sequence of facts as you, poor mortal knew it; and the other represents what History would have become if one single detail had been other than it was. . . . These infinite branchings make up the Unrealized Possibilities" (Maurois [1932] 1972, 52–53).

8. For a positive evaluation of thought experiments as tools of historical explanation, see De Mey and Weber 2003.

9. Elisabeth Wesseling resurrects the nineteenth-century term *Uchronie* to designate counterfactual historical narratives that "lie in a twilight zone between historiography and fiction. . . . Uchronian fantasy locates utopia in history, by imagining an apocryphal course of events, which clearly did not really take place, but which might have taken place" (1997, 204). It is not clear, however, whether she uses the term for all counterfactual historical narratives (as her examples would indicate) or means by it just a special kind of such narratives, namely, those that are manifestations of utopian thinking.

10. Churchill's game is not politically innocent. The interference of the British Empire in the American Civil War, in nineteenth-century world politics in general, and in the creation of the association is given much prominence. Moreover, we should recall that the creation of an English-speaking association became a major political goal (dream?) of the wartime British prime minister.

11. We know from section 3, above, that this idea was first suggested by Demandt (1993). Regrettably, Ferguson (1997) is not familiar with Demandt's work.

12. We can follow the same striving for well-founded restrictions in the work of counterfactual political scientists. Tetlock and Belkin advance "six normative criteria for judging counterfactual arguments," "six attributes of the ideal counterfactual thought exercise (where 'ideal' means most likely to contribute to the ultimate social-science goals of logically consistent, reasonably comprehensive and parsimonious, and rigorously testable explanations that integrate the idiographic and the nomothetic)" (1996, 17).

13. Ferguson points to several prominent historians and philosophers whose contributions stimulated the formulation of his method: Karl Popper, Charles Frankel, Patrick Gardiner, Isaiah Berlin, Marc Bloch, and last but not least, Hugh Trevor-Roper.

14. One kind of counterfactuals that seems to be excluded from Ferguson's set is alternative contraries to actual events that nobody considered, nobody anticipated. Ferguson is aware that such cases exist, but he argues that "we must attach equal importance to all the possibilities which contemporaries contemplated before the fact, and greater importance to these than to an outcome which they did not anticipate" (1997, 87). This "hierarchy" is a necessary consequence of Ferguson's method.

15. The focus of Fergusonian alternative history on short-term events accords with the general tendency of counterfactual thinking to change mainly "narrowly episodic elements" (Roese and Olson 1995a, 4). However, counterfactual history of *longue durée* still might have some future within the Fergusonian framework if a sufficient number of documents for the whole run of the alternative course is available. Josep Fontana writes: "If we examine European history in its passage from the Middle Ages to the modern period with eyes not clouded by mirages . . . , we discover that perhaps there was an alternative to the evolutionary path so far followed, a coherent programme for founding a more just and egalitarian society. . . . This would allow us to set up a model which would bring the so-called anomalies together and point towards a global interpretation of the grave social crisis which shook the continent. . . . It is not a question of something merely rustic . . . but of a broad current of critical culture in which members of the literate population played a part" (1995, 87). Similar alternatives existed, Fontana assures us, at the time of the Industrial Revolution. Confronting critically the popular view that "each change [is] an improvement, each new phase . . . progress," Fontana arrives at a view of history that is very similar to Ferguson's: "We shall . . . be able to replace it [the idea of automatic progress] by another better suited to analysing the complicated structure of the various trajectories which link up, separate, and cross over each other, of forks in the road at which it was possible to choose between several possible paths" (168).

16. Somewhat confusing is Megill's discussion of counterfactual history in his 2007 book, *Historical Knowledge, Historical Error.* On the one hand, he recognizes that "historians must engage in counterfactual reasoning," especially if they are interested in causal explanations. On the other hand, he dismisses most of counterfactual history, labeling it "exuberant." It "diverges radically from normal historical writing and research," asking such questions as "what might have resulted if Britain had intervened in the American Civil War, . . . or if Germany had invaded Britain in 1940." "This sort of counterfactual history [represented also

in Ferguson's collection] is . . . better called 'virtual history' to emphasize that it addresses no actual past—or 'imaginary history,' to emphasize its lack of groundedness." In contrast, "'restrained' counterfactual history involves an explicit canvassing of alternative possibilities that existed in a real past" (151). Specifically, it "moves from observed effect to hypothesized cause. . . . It starts out from an actual event, such as the English Civil War, and than looks back in time, canvassing how it might have come to pass that the Civil War might not have occurred (or might have occurred in a sharply different way)" (153). I have the impression that Meggill's "restrained" counterfactual history is only one special case of Ferguson's virtual history. His "canvassing of alternative possibilities that existed in a real past" is just a reformulation of Ferguson's main epistemological principle.

# WORKS CITED


Abrams, M. H. 1977. "The Deconstructive Angel." *Critical Inquiry* 3:425–38.

Adams, Ernest. 1975. *The Logic of Conditionals: An Application of Probability to Deductive Logic.* Dordrecht, Holland: Reidel.

Adams, Robert M. 1979. "Theories of Actuality." In Loux, ed., 1979, 190–209.

Allén, Sture, ed. 1989. *Possible Worlds in Humanities, Arts, and Sciences: Proceedings of Nobel Symposium 65.* Berlin: de Gruyter.

Amis, Kingsley. 1976. *Alteration.* London: Cape.

Ankersmit, Frank, and Hans Kellner, eds. 1995. *A New Philosophy of History.* Chicago: University of Chicago Press.

Appleby, Joyce, Elizabeth Covington, David Hoyt, Michael Latham, and Allison Sneider, eds. 1996. *Knowledge and Postmodernism in Historical Perspective.* New York: Routledge.

Appleby, Joyce, Lynn Hunt, and Margaret Jacob. 1994. *Telling the Truth about History.* New York: Norton.

Arnold, Heinz Ludwig, and Volker Sinemus, eds. 1973. *Grundzüge der Literatur- und Sprachwissenschaft.* Vol. 1, *Literaturwissenschaft.* Munich: Deutscher Taschenbuch Verlag.

Attridge, Derek. 1992. Introduction to Derrida 1992.

Austin, J. L. 1962. *How to Do Things with Words.* Cambridge, MA: Harvard University Press.

———. 1971. "Performative-Constative." In *The Philosophy of Language,* ed. J. R. Searle, 13–22. Oxford: Oxford University Press.

Barnes, Harry Elmer. 1962. *A History of Historical Writing.* 2nd ed. New York: Dover.

Baron, Salo W. 1986. *The Contemporary Relevance of History: A Study in Approaches and Methods.* New York: Columbia University Press.

Barthes, Roland. 1957. *Mythologies.* Paris: Seuil.

———. 1966. "Introduction à l'analyse structurale des récits." *Communications* 8:1–27.

———. 1967. "Le discours de l'histoire." *Social Science Information—Studies in Semiotics/Recherches Sémiotiques,* 65–75. Translated by S. Bann as "The Discourse of History" in *Comparative Criticism: A Yearbook*, ed. E. S. Shaffer (Cambridge: Cambridge University Press, 1981), 3:7–20.

Baumgartner, Hans Michael. 1975. "Narrative Struktur und Objektivität: Wahrheitskriterien im historischen Wissen." In *Historische Objektivität: Aufsätze zur Geschichtstheorie*, ed. J. Rüsen, 48–67. Göttingen: Vandenhoeck & Ruprecht.

Bell, J. S. 1989. "Six Possible Worlds of Quantum Mechanics." In Allén, ed., 1989, 359–73.

Belloc, Hilaire. [1932] 1972. "If Drouet's Cart Had Stuck." In Squire, ed., [1932] 1972, 79–112.

Benhabib, Seyla. 1996. "Feminism and the Question of Postmodernism." In Appleby et al., eds., 1996, 540–54.

Berenson, Edward. 1992. *The Trial of Madame Caillaux*. Berkeley: University of California Press.

Berkhofer, Robert F., Jr. 1997. *Beyond the Great Story: History as Text and Discourse*. Cambridge, MA: Harvard University Press.

Bertens, Hans. 1997. "The Debate on Postmodernism." In Bertens and Fokkema, eds., 1997, 3–14.

Bertens, Hans, and Douwe Fokkema, eds. 1997. *International Postmodernism: Theory and Practice*. Amsterdam: Benjamins.

Bindoff, S. T. 1962. "Political History." In Finberg, ed., 1962, 1–15.

Bloom, Harold, ed. 2002. *Modern Critical Views: E. L. Doctorow*. Philadelphia: Chelsea House.

Boethius, Henning. 1973. "Poetik." In Arnold and Sinemus, eds., 1973, 115–33.

Bradbury, Malcolm. 2000. *To the Hermitage*. London: Picador.

Bradley, Raymond, and Norman Swartz. 1979. *Possible Worlds: An Introduction to Logic and Its Philosophy*. Oxford: Blackwell.

Braudel, Fernand. 1980. *On History*. Trans. Sarah Matthews. Chicago: University of Chicago Press.

Breslauer, George W. 1996. "Counterfactual Reasoning in Western Studies of Soviet Politics and Foreign Relations." In Tetlock and Belkin, eds., 1996, 71–94.

Bueno de Mesquita, Bruce. 1996. "Counterfactuals and International Affairs: Some Insights from Game Theory." In Tetlock and Belkin, eds., 1996, 211–29.

Bulhof, Johannes. 1999. "What If? Modality and History." *History and Theory* 38:145–68.

Burke, Peter. 1992a. "History of Events and the Revival of Narrative." In Burke, ed., 1992, 233–48.

———. 1992b. "Overture: The New History, Its Past and Its Future." In Burke, ed., 1992, 1–23.

———, ed. 1992. *New Perspectives on Historical Writing*. University Park: Pennsylvania State University Press.

Burleigh, Michael. 1997. "Nazi Europe: What If Nazi Germany Had Defeated the Soviet Union?" In Ferguson, ed., 1997, 321–47.

Buxton, Jackie. 2001. "'What's Love Got to Do with It?': Postmodernism and *Possession*." In *Essays on the Fiction of A. S. Byatt: Imagining the Real*, ed. Alexa Alter and Michael J. Noble, 89–104. Westport, CT: Greenwood.

Byatt, A. S. 1990. *Possession: A Romance*. London: Chatto & Windus.

Campbell, Jane. 2004. *A. S. Byatt and the Heliotropic Imagination*. Waterloo, ON: Wilfrid Laurier University Press.

Carr, David. 1986a. "Narrative and the Real World." *History and Theory* 25: 117–31.

———. 1986b. *Time, Narrative, and History*. Bloomington: Indiana University Press.

Carr, E. H. 1964. *What Is History?* Harmondsworth: Penguin.

Carrard, Philippe. 1995. "Theory of a Practice: Historical Enunciation and the *Annales* School." In Ankersmit and Kellner, eds., 1995, 108–26.

Cederman, Lars-Erik. 1996. "Rerunning History: Counterfactual Simulation in World Politics." In Tetlock and Belkin, eds., 1996, 247–67.

Chartier, Roger. 1995. "The World as Representation." In Revel and Hunt, eds., 1995, 544–58.

Châtelet, François. 1962. *La naissance de l'histoire: La formation de la pensée historienne en Grèce*. Paris: Editions de Minuit.

Chisholm, Roderick M. 1981. *The First Person: An Essay on Reference and Intentionality*. Brighton, Sussex: Harvester.

Churchill, Winston. [1932] 1972. "If Lee Did Not Win the Battle of Gettysburg." In Squire, ed., [1932] 1972, 175–96.

———. 1949. *Their Finest Hour*. Boston: Houghton Mifflin.

Cohn, Dorrit. 1989. "Fictional versus Historical Lives: Borderlines and Borderline Cases." *Journal of Narrative Technique* 19:3–24.

———. 1999. *The Distinction of Fiction*. Baltimore: Johns Hopkins University Press.

Collingwood, Robin George. 1993. *The Idea of History*. Ed. Jan van der Dussen. Oxford: Clarendon.

Connor, Steven. [1989] 1997. *Postmodernist Culture: An Introduction to Theories of the Contemporary*. Repr. Oxford: Blackwell.

Coste, Didier. 1989. *Narrative as Communication*. Minneapolis: University of Minnesota Press.

Cowley, Robert, ed. 2003. *What Ifs? of American History: Eminent Historians Imagine What Might Have Been*. New York: Putnam's Sons.

Cresswell, M. J. 1988. *Semantical Essays: Possible Worlds and Their Rivals.* Dordrecht, Holland: Kluwer.

Crowell, Steven G. 1998. "Mixed Messages: The Heterogeneity of Historical Discourse." *History and Theory* 37:220–44.

Culler, Jonathan. 1982. *On Deconstruction: Theory and Criticism after Structuralism.* Ithaca, NY: Cornell University Press.

Curthoyse, Ann, and John Docker. 2005. *Is History Fiction?* Ann Arbor: University of Michigan Press.

Dällenbach, Lucien. 1984. "Reading as Suture (Problems of Reception of the Fragmentary Text: Balzac and Claude Simon)." *Style* 18:196–206.

Demandt, Alexander. 1993. *History That Never Happened: A Treatise on the Question, What Would Have Happened If . . . ?* Trans. Colin D. Thomson. 3rd ed. Jefferson, NC: McFarland.

De Mey, Tim, and Erik Weber. 2003. "Explanation and Thought Experiments in History." *History and Theory* 42:28–38.

Dening, Greg. 2004. "Performing on the Beaches of the Mind: An Essay." In Jenkins and Munslow, eds., 2004, 117–34.

Derrida, Jacques. 1992. *Acts of Literature.* Ed. Derek Attridge. New York: Routledge.

———. 1996. "Structure, Sign, and Play in the Discourse of the Human Sciences." In Appleby et al., eds., 1996, 437–48. Originally published in *Writing and Difference,* trans. Alan Bass (Chicago: University of Chicago Press, 1978), 278–95.

D'haen, Theo, and Hans Bertens, eds. 1988. *Postmodern Fiction in Europe and the Americas.* Amsterdam: Rodopi.

Dick, Philip K. 1962. *The Man in the High Castle.* New York: Putnam.

Doctorow, E. L. 1974. *Ragtime.* New York: Random House.

———. 1999. *Conversations with E. L. Doctorow.* Jackson: University Press of Mississippi.

Doležel, Lubomír. 1973. *Narrative Modes in Czech Literature.* Toronto: University of Toronto Press.

———. 1980. "A Short Note on a Long Subject: Literary Style." In *Voz'mi na radost': To Honour Jeanne van der Eng-Liedmeier,* 1–7. Amsterdam: Slavic Seminar.

———. 1990. *Occidental Poetics: Tradition and Progress.* Lincoln: University of Nebraska Press.

———. 1995. "Fictional Worlds: Density, Gaps, and Inference." *Style* 25:201–14.

———. 1998. *Heterocosmica: Fiction and Possible Worlds.* Baltimore: Johns Hopkins University Press.

———. 2000. "Poststructuralism: A View from Charles Bridge." *Poetics Today* 21:634–51.

Eco, Umberto. 1983. *Postscript to "The Name of the Rose."* San Diego: Harcourt Brace Jovanovich.

———. 1989a. "Report on Session 3: Literature and Arts." In Allén, ed., 1989, 343–55.

———. 1989b. "Small Worlds." *VS. Versus* 52–53:53–70.

———. 1994. *Six Walks in the Fictional Woods.* Cambridge, MA: Harvard University Press.

Ellis, John M. 1989. *Against Deconstruction.* Princeton, NJ: Princeton University Press.

Fay, Brian. 1998. "Introduction: The Linguistic Turn and Beyond in Contemporary Theory of History." In Fay, Pomper, and Vann, eds., 1998, 1–12.

———. 2003. "Environmental History: Nature at Work." *History and Theory* 42:1–4.

Fay, Brian, Philip Pomper, and Richard T. Vann, eds. 1998. *History and Theory: Contemporary Readings.* London: Blackwell.

Fearon, James D. 1991. "Counterfactuals and Hypothesis Testing in Political Science." *World Politics* 43:169–95.

———. 1996. "Causes and Counterfactuals in Social Science: Exploring an Analogy between Cellular Automata and Historical Processes." In Tetlock and Belkin, eds., 1996, 39–67.

Ferguson, Niall. 1997. "Introduction: Virtual History; Towards a Chaotic Theory of the Past." In Ferguson, ed., 1997, 1–90.

———, ed. 1997. *Virtual History: Alternatives and Counterfactuals.* London: Picador.

Feuer, Kathryn B. 1996. *Tolstoy and the Genesis of "War and Peace."* Ithaca, NY: Cornell University Press.

Finberg, H. P. R., ed. 1962. *Approaches to History: A Symposium.* London: Routledge & Kegan Paul.

Fisher, Herbert A. L. "If Napoleon Had Escaped to America." In Squire, ed., [1932] 1972, 113–42.

Fogel, R. 1964. *Railroads and American Economic Growth: Essays in Econometric History.* Baltimore: Johns Hopkins University Press.

Fokkema, Douwe. 1987. "Concluding Observations: Is There a Future for Research on Modernism?" In *Exploring Postmodernism,* ed. Matei Calinescu and Douwe Fokkema, 233–41. Amsterdam: Benjamins.

———. 1997. "The Semiotics of Literary Postmodernism." In Bertens and Fokkema, eds., 1997, 15–42.

Foley, Barbara. 1986. *Telling the Truth: The Theory and Practice of Documentary Fiction.* Ithaca, NY: Cornell University Press.

Fontana i Lazaro, Josep. 1995. *The Distorted Past: A Reinterpretation of Europe.* Trans. Colin Smith. Oxford: Blackwell.

Fowles, John. 1977. *The French Lieutenant's Woman.* London: Cape.

Frege, Gottlob. [1892] 1969. "Über Sinn und Bedeutung." In *Funktion, Begriff, Bedeutung: Fünf logische Studien,* ed. Günther Patzig, 40–65. 3rd ed. Göttingen: Vandenhoeck & Ruprecht, 1969. Translated as "On Sense and Reference" in *Translations from the Philosophical Writings of Gottlob Frege,* ed. and trans. Peter Geach and Max Black (Oxford: Blackwell, 1980), 56–78. Reprinted in Zabeeh, Klemke, and Jacobson, eds., 1974, 118–40.

Freundlieb, Dieter. 1988. "Semiotic Idealism." *Poetics Today* 9:807–41.

Friedlander, Saul, ed. 1992. *Probing the Limits of Representation: Nazism and "the Final Solution."* Cambridge, MA: Harvard University Press.

Frye, Northrop. 1957. *Anatomy of Criticism.* Princeton, NJ: Princeton University Press.

Gallie, Walter Bryce. 1964. *Philosophy and Historical Understanding.* London: Chatto & Windus.

Gaskell, Ivan. 1992. "History of Images." In Burke, ed., 1992, 168–92.

Gauthier, Tim S. 2006. *Narrative Desire and Historical Reparations: A. S. Byatt, Ian McEwan, Salmon Rushdie.* New York: Routledge.

Gibbon, Edward. [1909] 1974. *The History of the Decline and Fall of the Roman Empire.* Ed. J. B. Bury. 7 vols. Repr. New York: AMS Press. Originally published in 1737–94.

Ginzburg, Carlo. 1992. *The Cheese and the Worms: The Cosmos of a Sixteenth-Century Miller.* Baltimore: Johns Hopkins University Press.

Goldhagen, Daniel. 1996. *Hitler's Willing Executioners: Ordinary Germans and the Holocaust.* New York: Knopf.

Goodman, Nelson. 1978. *Ways of Worldmaking.* Indianapolis: Hackett.

Gross, David S. 1986. "Doctorow, E. L." In McCaffery, ed., 1986, 339–42.

Guedalla, Philip. [1932] 1972. "If the Moors in Spain Had Won." In Squire, ed., [1932] 1972, 1–20.

Harris, Robert. 1992. *Fatherland.* London: Hutchinson.

Harter, Carol C., and James R. Thompson. 1990. *E. L. Doctorow.* Boston: Twayne.

Hawthorn, Geoffrey. 1991. *Plausible Worlds: Possibility and Understanding in History and Social Sciences.* Cambridge: Cambridge University Press.

Heintz, John. 1979. "Reference and Inference in Fiction." *Poetics* 8:85–99.

Hintikka, Jaakko. 1975. *The Intentions of Intentionality and Other New Models for Modalities.* Dordrecht, Holland: Reidel.

———. 1989. "Exploring Possible Worlds." In Allén, ed., 1989, 52–73.

Howe, Irving. 1978. *Leon Trotsky.* New York: Viking.

Hughes-Warrington, Marnie. 2000. *Fifty Key Thinkers on History.* London: Routledge.

Hutcheon, Linda. 1988. *A Poetics of Postmodernism: History, Theory, Fiction.* New York: Routledge.

———. 1989. *The Politics of Postmodernism.* New York: Routledge.

Iggers, Georg G. 1997. *Historiography in the Twentieth Century: From Scientific Objectivity to the Postmodern Challenge.* Hanover, NH: Wesleyan University Press.

Jakobson, Roman. 1957. "Shifters, Verbal Categories, and the Russian Verb." In *Russian and Slavic Grammar: Studies 1931–1981,* ed. L. R. Waugh and Morris Halle, 41–58. Berlin: Mouton.

James, P. D. 1997. *A Certain Justice.* London: Faber & Faber.

Jenkins, Keith. 1997. "Introduction: On Being Open about Our Closures." In Jenkins, ed., 1997, 1–30.

———, ed. 1997. *The Postmodern History Reader.* London: Routledge.

———. 2000. "A Postmodern Reply to Perez Zagorin." *History and Theory* 39:181–200.

Jenkins, Keith, and Alun Munslow. 2004. Introduction to Jenkins and Munslow, eds., 2004.

———, eds. 2004. *The Nature of History Reader.* London: Routledge.

Kahneman, Daniel. 1995. "Varieties of Counterfactual Thinking." In Roese and Olson, eds., 1995, 375–96.

Kammen, Michael, ed. 1980. *The Past before Us: Contemporary Historical Writing in the United States.* Ithaca, NY: Cornell University Press.

———. 1980. "The State of the Discipline in the United States." In Kammen, ed., 1980.

Kasimatis, Margaret, and Gary L. Wells. 1995. "Individual Differences in Counterfactual Thinking." In Roese and Olson, eds., 1995, 81–101.

Keegan, John. 1995. *The Battle for History: Re-Fighting World War II.* London: Pimlico.

Kellner, Hans. 1997. "'Never Again' Is Now." In Jenkins, ed., 1997, 397–412.

Kelly, Kathleen Coyne. 1996. *A. S. Byatt.* New York: Twayne.

Kibédi-Varga, Aron. 1988. "Narrative and Postmodernity in France." In D'haen and Bertens, eds., 1988, 27–43.

Kirkham, Richard L. 1992. *Theories of Truth: A Critical Introduction.* Cambridge, MA: MIT Press.

Kripke, Saul A. 1963. "Semantical Considerations on Modal Logic." *Acta Philosophica Fennica* 16: 83–94. Reprinted in Zabeeh, Klemke, and Jacobson, eds., 1974, 803–14.

———. 1980. *Naming and Necessity.* Cambridge, MA: Harvard University Press.

LaCapra, Dominick, and Steven Kaplan, eds. 1982. *Modern European Intellec-*

*tual History: Reappraisals and New Perspectives.* Ithaca, NY: Cornell University Press.

Lane, Michael, ed. 1970. *Structuralism: A Reader.* London: Cape.

Lang, Berel. 1990. *Act and Idea in the Nazi Genocide.* Chicago: University of Chicago Press.

———. 1997. "Is It Possible to Misrepresent the Holocaust?" In Jenkins, ed., 1997, 426–33.

———. 1998. "Is it Possible to Misrepresent the Holocaust?" In Fay, Pomper, and Vann, eds., 1998, 245–50.

Le Goff, Jacques. 1992. *History and Memory.* Trans. Steven Rendall and Elizabeth Claman. New York: Columbia University Press.

Le Goff, Jacques, and Pierre Nora. 1995. "Constructing the Past." In Revel and Hunt, eds., 1995, 321–27.

Le Roy Ladurie, Emmanuel. 1980. *Carnival in Romans.* Trans. Mary Freney. New York: Braziller.

Lewis, David K. 1973. *Counterfactuals.* Cambridge, MA: Harvard University Press.

———. 1983. *Philosophical Papers.* Vol. 1. New York: Oxford University Press.

———. 1986. *On the Plurality of Worlds.* Oxford: Blackwell.

Loux, Michael J., ed. 1979. *The Possible and the Actual: Readings in the Metaphysics of Modality.* Ithaca, NY: Cornell University Press.

Lucas, Colin. 1985. Introduction to *Constructing the Past: Essays in Historical Methodology,* ed. Jacques Le Goff and Pierre Nora, 1–11. Cambridge: Cambridge University Press; Paris: Editions de la Maison des sciences de l'homme.

Ludwig, Emil. "If the Emperor Frederick Had Not Had Cancer." In Squire, ed., [1932] 1972, 319–20.

Lycan, William G. 1979. "The Trouble with Possible Worlds." In Loux, ed., 1979, 274–316.

Mandelbaum, Maurice. 1938. *The Problem of Historical Knowledge: An Answer to Relativism.* New York: Liveright.

Martin, Raymond. 1998. "Progress in Historical Studies." In Fay, Pomper, and Vann, eds., 1998, 377–403.

Martin, Thomas L. 2005. *Poiesis and Possible Worlds: A Study in Modality and Literary Theory.* Toronto: University of Toronto Press.

Maurois, André. [1932] 1972. "If Louis XVI Had Had an Atom of Firmness." In Squire, ed., [1932] 1972, 49–78.

McCaffery, Larry. 1986. Introduction to McCaffery, ed., 1986, xi–xxviii.

———, ed. 1986. *Postmodern Fiction: A Bio-Bibliographical Guide.* New York: Greenwood.

McCullagh, C. Behan. 1987. "The Truth of Historical Narratives." In *History and Theory,* suppl. 26, *The Representation of Historical Events,* 33–40.
———. 1998. *The Truth of History.* London: Routledge.
McHale, Brian. 1987. *Postmodernist Fiction.* London: Routledge.
McKnight, Edgar V. 1994. "Alternative History: The Development of a Literary Genre." PhD diss., University of North Carolina at Chapel Hill.
McNeill, J. R. 2003. "Observations on the Nature and Culture in Environmental History." *History and Theory* 42:5–43.
Megill, Allan. 1995. "'Grand Narrative' and the Discipline of History." In Ankersmit and Kellner, eds., 1995, 151–73.
———. 2007. *Historical Knowledge, Historical Error: A Contemporary Guide to Practice.* Chicago: University of Chicago Press.
Miller, J. Hillis. 1976. "Stevens' Rock and Criticism as Cure." *Georgia Review* 30:5-33, 330-48.
———. 1980. "The Figure in the Carpet." *Poetics Today* 1:107–18.
———. 1980–81. "A Guest in the House: Reply to Shlomith Rimmon-Kenan." *Poetics Today* 2:180–91.
———. 1985. "Topography and Tropography in Thomas Hardy's *In Front of the Landscape.*" In *Identity of the Literary Text,* ed. M. J. Valdés and O. Miller, 73–91. Toronto: University of Toronto Press.
Miller, Richard B. 1990. "There Is Nothing Magical about Possible Worlds." *Mind* 99: 453–57.
Mink, Louis. 1998. "History and Fiction as Modes of Comprehension." In Fay, Pomper, and Vann, eds., 1998, 121–36.
Moore, Ward. 1953. *Bring the Jubilee.* New York: Farrar, Strauss & Young.
Morris, Christopher D. 2002. "Illusions of Demystification in Ragtime." In Bloom, ed., 2002, 91–104.
Munslow, Alun. 1997. *Deconstructing History.* London: Routledge.
———. 2000. *The Routledge Companion to Historical Studies.* London: Routledge.
Munslow, Alun, and Robert A. Rosenstone, eds. 2004. *Experiments in Rethinking History.* London: Routledge.
Murray, Janet H. 1997. *Hamlet on the Holodeck: The Future of Narrative in Cyberspace.* New York: Free Press.
Nesselroth, Peter W. 1999. "From De-automatization to Undecidability: Jan Mukařovský's Legacy." In *Jan Mukařovský and the Prague School,* ed. V. Macura and H. Schmid, 26–33. Potsdam: Universität Potsdam; Prague: Ústav pro českou literaturu AV ČR.
———. 2007. "Playing Doubles: Derrida's Writing." *Semiotica* 166:427–44.
Noiriel, Gérard. 1996. *Sur la "crise" de l'histoire.* Paris: Belin.

———. 1998. *Qu'est-ce que l'histoire contemporaine?* Paris: Hachette.

Nolt, John Eric. 1986. "What Are Possible Worlds?" *Mind* 95:432–45.

Norris, Christopher. 1988. *Deconstruction and the Interests of Theory*. London: Pinter.

Pavel, Thomas G. 1975–76. "Possible Worlds in Literary Semantics." *Journal of Aesthetics and Art Criticism* 34:165–76.

———. 1986. *Fictional Worlds*. Cambridge, MA: Harvard University Press.

———. 1989. *The Feud of Language: A History of Structuralist Thought*. Oxford: Blackwell.

Plantinga, Alvin. 1974. *The Nature of Necessity*. Oxford: Clarendon.

Poster, Mark. 1997. *Cultural History and Postmodernity: Disciplinary Readings and Challenges*. New York: Columbia University Press.

Rajneke, Julija C. 2002. *Istoričeskij roman postmodernizma (Austria, Velikobritanija, Germanija, Russia)* [Historical Novel of Postmodernism: Austria, Great Britain, Germany, Russia]. Moscow: Institut slavjanovedenija.

Rees, Martin J. 1989. "Our Universe and Others: The Limits of Space, Time and Physics." In Allén, ed., 1989, 396–416.

———. 1997. *Before the Beginning: Our Universe and Others*. Reading, MA: Addison-Wesley.

Rennhak, Katharina. 2002. *Sprachkonzeptionen im metahistorischem Roman: Diskurspezifische Ausprägungen des Linguistic Turn in Critical Theory, Geschichtstheorie und Geschichtsfiktion (1970–1990)*. Munich: Fink.

Rescher, Nicholas. 1969. *Essays in Philosophical Analysis*. Pittsburg: Pittsburg University Press.

———. 1973. *The Coherence Theory of Truth*. Oxford: Clarendon.

———. 1975. *A Theory of Possibility: A Constructivistic and Conceptualist Account of Possible Individuals and Possible Worlds*. Oxford: Blackwell.

Rescher, Nicholas, and Robert Brandom. 1980. *The Logic of Inconsistency: A Study in Non-Standard Possible-World Semantics and Ontology*. Oxford: Blackwell.

Revel, Jacques. 1995. "Microanalysis and Deconstruction of the Social." In Revel and Hunt, eds., 1995, 492–502.

Revel, Jacques, and Lynn Hunt, eds. 1995. *Histories: French Constructions of the Past*. New York: New Press.

Ricoeur, Paul. 1984–88. *Time and Narrative*. 3 vols. Vols. 1 and 2 trans. K. McLaughlin and D. Pellauer; vol. 3 trans. K. Blamey and D. Pellauer. Chicago: University of Chicago Press. Originally published as *Temps et récit*, 3 vols. (Paris: Seuil, 1983–85).

Rimmon-Kenan, Shlomith. 1980–81. "Deconstructive Reflections on Deconstruction: In Reply to Hillis Miller." *Poetics Today* 2:185–88.

Rodiek, Christoph. 1997. *Erfurdene Vergangenheit: Kontrafaktische Geschichtsdarstellung (Uchronie) in der Literatur.* Frankfurt am Main: Klostermann.

Roese, Neal J., and James M. Olson. 1995a. "Counterfactual Thinking: A Critical Overview." In Roese and Olson, eds., 1995, 1–55.

———. 1995b. "Functions of Counterfactual Thinking." In Roese and Olson, eds., 1995, 169–97.

———, eds. 1995. *What Might Have Been: The Social Psychology of Counterfactual Thinking.* Mahwah, NJ: Lawrence Erlbaum.

Ronen, Ruth. 1994. *Possible Worlds in Literary Theory.* Cambridge: Cambridge University Press.

Rose, Gillian. 1984. *Dialectic of Nihilism: Postsructuralism and Law.* Oxford: Blackwell.

Rosenfeld, Gavriel. 2002. "Why Do We Ask 'What If?' Reflections on the Functions of Alternate History." *History and Theory* 41:90–103.

Rosenstone, Robert A. 2004. "Introduction: Practice and Theory." In Munslow and Rosenstone, eds., 2004, 1–5.

Rousso, Henry. 1995. "The Vichy Syndrome: History and Memory since 1944." In Revel and Hunt, eds., 1995, 644–49.

Ryan, Marie-Laure. 1984. "Fiction as Logical, Ontological and Illocutionary Issue." *Style* 18:121–39.

———. 1991. *Possible Worlds, Artificial Intelligence, and Narrative Theory.* Bloomington: Indiana University Press.

———. 2006. "From Parallel Universes to Possible Worlds: Ontological Pluralism in Physics, Narratology and Narrative." *Poetics Today* 27:633–74.

Saunders, Corinne. 2004. Introduction to *A Companion to Romance: From Classical to Contemporary,* ed. Corinne Saunders. Malden, MA: Blackwell.

Savan, David. 1983. "Toward a Refutation of Semiotic Idealism." *Recherches sémiotiques/Semiotic Inquiry* 3:1–8.

Schama, Simon. 1989. *Citizens: A Chronicle of the French Revolution.* London: Viking.

———. 1991. *Dead Certainties (Unwarranted Speculations).* New York: Knopf.

———. 1996. *Landscape and Memory.* Toronto: Vintage Canada.

———. 1999. *Rembrandt's Eyes.* Toronto: Random House.

Schulz, Bruno. 1977. "Sanatorium under the Sign of the Hourglass." In *Sanatorium under the Sign of the Hourglass,* trans. C. Wieniewska, 112–40. New York: Walker.

Seelau, Eric P., Sheila M. Seelau, Gary L. Wells, and Paul D. Windschitl. 1995. "Counterfactual Constraints." In Roese and Olson, eds., 1995, 57–79.

Semino, Elena. 1997. *Language and World Creation in Poems and Other Texts.* New York: Longman.

Sherman, Steven J., and Allen R. McConnell. 1995. "Dysfunctional Implications of Counterfactual Thinking: When Alternatives to Reality Fail Us." In Roese and Olson, eds., 1995, 199–231.

Shklovsky, Viktor. [1928] 1970. *Material i stil' v romane L'va Tolstogo "Vojna i mir"* [Material and Style in Lev Tolstoy's Novel *War and Peace*]. Repr. The Hague: Mouton.

Simon, Bryant. 1998. *A Fabric of Defeat: The Politics of South Carolina Millhands, 1910–1948*. Chapel Hill: University of North Carolina Press.

———. 2004. "Narrating a Southern Tragedy: Historical Facts and Historical Fictions." In Munslow and Rosenstone, eds., 2004, 156–82.

Slinin, J. A. 1967. "Teorija modal'nostej v sovremennoj logike" [Theory of Modalities in Contemporary Logic]. In *Logičeskaja semantika i modal'naja logika*, ed. P. V. Tavanec, 119–47. Moscow: Nauka.

Spiegel, Gabrielle M. 2005. Introduction to Spiegel, ed., 2005, 1–31.

———, ed. 2005. *Practicing History: New Directions in Historical Writing after the Linguistic Turn*. New York: Routledge.

Squire, J. C., ed. [1932] 1972. *If It Had Happened Otherwise: Lapses into Imaginary History*. 2nd ed. London: Sidgwick & Jackson.

Stalnaker, Robert C. 1984. *Inquiry*. Cambridge, MA: MIT Press.

Stevenson, David. 2004. *Cataclysm: The First World War as Political Tragedy*. New York: Basic Books.

Sukenick, Ronald. 1975. *98.6*. New York: Fiction Collective.

Suleiman, Susan Rubin. 2000. "Problems of Memory and Factuality in Recent Holocaust Memoirs." *Poetics Today* 21:543–59.

Swift, Graham. 1984. *Waterland*. London: Heinemann.

Tetlock, Philip E., and Aaron Belkin. 1996. "Counterfactual Thought Experiments in World Politics: Logical, Methodological, and Psychological Perspectives." In Tetlock and Belkin, eds., 1996, 1–38.

———, eds. 1996. *Counterfactual Thought Experiments in World Politics: Logical, Methodological, and Psychological Perspectives*. Princeton, NJ: Princeton University Press.

Thiher, Allen. 1990. "Postmodern Fiction and History." In *History and Post-war Writing*, ed. Theo D'haen and Hans Bertens, 9–31. Amsterdam: Rodopi.

Todd, Richard. 1988. "Confrontation with Convention: On the Character of British Postmodernist Fiction." In D'haen and Bertens eds., 1988, 115–25.

Traill, Nancy H. 1996. *Possible Worlds of the Fantastic: The Rise of Paranormal Fiction*. Toronto: University or Toronto Press.

Trevor-Roper, Hugh. 1969. *The Romantic Movement and the Study of History*. London: Athlone.

———. 1976. *A Hidden Life: The Enigma of Sir Edmund Backhouse.* London: Macmillan.
———. 1980. *History and Imagination.* Oxford: Clarendon.
Ulmer, Gregory L. 1985. *Applied Grammatology: Post(e)-Pedagogy from Jacques Derrida to Joseph Beuys.* Baltimore: Johns Hopkins University Press.
Vann, Richard T. 1995. "Turning Linguistic: History and Theory and *History and Theory,* 1960–1975." In Ankersmit and Kellner, eds., 1995, 40–69.
———. 1998. "The Reception of Hayden White." *History and Theory* 37:143–61.
Veyne, Paul. 1984. *Writing History: Essay on Epistemology.* Trans. Mina Moore-Rinvolucri. Middletown, CT: Wesleyan University Press. Originally published in French as *Comment on écrit l'histoire* (Paris: Seuil, 1971).
Vidal-Naquet, Pierre. 2005. *Les assassins de la mémoire: "Un Eichman de papier" et autres essais sur le révisionism.* Paris: Découverte.
Weber, Steven. 1996. "Counterfactuals, Past and Future." In Tetlock and Belkin, eds., 1996, 268–88.
Wesseling, Elisabeth. 1991. *Writing History as a Prophet: Postmodernist Innovations of the Historical Novel.* Amsterdam: Benjamins.
———. 1997. "Historical Fiction: Utopia in History." In Bertens and Fokkema, eds., 1997, 203–11.
White, Hayden. 1973. *Metahistory: The Historical Imagination in Nineteenth-Century Europe.* Baltimore: Johns Hopkins University Press.
———. 1978. *Tropics of Discourse: Essays in Cultural Criticism.* Baltimore: Johns Hopkins University Press.
———. 1987. *The Content of the Form: Narrative Discourse and Historical Representation.* Baltimore: Johns Hopkins University Press.
———. 1992. "Historical Emplotment and the Problem of Truth." In Friedlander, ed., 1992, 37–53.
———. 1999. *Figural Realism: Studies in the Mimesis Effect.* Baltimore: Johns Hopkins University Press.
Williams, John. 1996. *Fiction as False Document: The Reception of E. L. Doctorow in the Postmodern Age.* Columbia, SC: Camden House.
Windschuttle, Keith. 1996. *The Killing of History: How Literary Critics and Social Theorists Are Murdering Our Past.* New York: Free Press.
Wolterstorff, Nicholas. 1980. *Works and Worlds of Art.* Oxford: Clarendon.
Woods, John Hayden. 1974. *The Logic of Fiction: A Philosophical Sounding of Deviant Logic.* The Hague: Mouton.
Woods, Michael. 1997. *Conditionals.* Ed. David Wiggins. Oxford: Clarendon.
Wright, Georg H. von. 1968. *Essay in Deontic Logic and the General Theory of Action.* Amsterdam: North-Holland.

———. 1974. *Causality and Determinism.* New York: Columbia University Press.

Yagisawa, Takashi. 1988. "Beyond Possible Worlds." *Philosophical Studies* 53:175–204.

Zabeeh, Farhang, E. D. Klemke, and Arthur Jacobson, eds. 1974. *Readings in Semantics.* Urbana: University of Illinois Press.

Zagorin, Perez. 1999. "History, the Referent, and Narrative: Reflections on Postmodernism Now." *History and Theory* 38:1–24.

———. 2000. "Rejoinder to a Postmodernist." *History and Theory* 39:201–9.

# INDEX